ORIENTAL VEGETARIAN COOKING

Other titles in this series

ORIENTAL

VEGETARIAN COOKING

GAIL DUFF

Illustrated by Jenni Rodger

HEALING ARTS PRESS

Rochester, Vermont

Healing Arts Press
One Park Street
Rochester, Vermont 05767

First U.S. Edition

Copyright © 1986, 1989 by Gail Duff

Library of Congress Cataloging-in-Publication Data

Duff, Gail.
  Oriental vegetarian cooking.
  Includes index.
  1. Vegetarian cookery. 2. Cookery, Oriental.
I. Title.
TX837.D8   1988   641.5´636   88-32902
ISBN 0-89281-344-X

Printed and bound in the United States

10 9 8 7 6 5 4 3 2

Healing Arts Press is a division of Inner Traditions International, Ltd.

Distributed to the book trade in Canada by Book Center, Inc., Montreal, Quebec

Distributed to the health food trade in Canada by Alive Books, Toronto and Vancouver

Contents

Introduction

The exotic food of the East is no longer the tantalizing mystery it once was. For some years now the ingredients necessary for preparing meals with an eastern flavour have been increasingly available in the West. This is especially true in those shops catering to wholefood eaters and vegetarians. In the West these have pioneered in the use of miso, tamari or shoyu sauce and sea vegetables. Rice, the brown kind of course, has for a long time featured more in western vegetarian meals than in nonvegetarian ones. Vegetarians are more used to using tofu (or bean curd) than are those on mixed diets, and vegetarian dishes call for a frequent but subtle use of spices.

Put all these factors together and the preparing of eastern-style meals in the vegetarian kitchen is the next logical step. The flavours may at first seem a little exotic and the preparations unfamiliar, but eastern cooking is not difficult. It can, in fact, be a pure delight, since you are not only producing meals with a superb flavour but also those which look extremely attractive and which include a wide variety of textures.

Eastern cooking encompasses the varied cooking styles of several different regions. Most familiar in the West is the Chinese style. The sweet-and-sour dishes from Canton are perhaps the first to spring to mind, but look to the north of China and there are dishes spiced with chilli and given a nutty flavour with sesame paste.

The Chinese make a speciality of cutting, cooking and serving all types of vegetable dishes. Even their meat dishes frequently contain more vegetables than meat. Some Chinese are Buddhist or Taoist and for these meat is completely forbidden. Dairy products are little used in China, and so protein is mainly derived from bean curd. Many are the tantalizing dishes that Buddhist cooks have devised by using this one basic ingredient. Nuts are occasionally used in China, and there are also some superb egg dishes. Combine these with rice, noodles or steamed breads and buns, and the vegetarian has a good many dishes from which to choose.

Although the cooking of Japan is based very much on seafood, there are still many unusual vegetarian dishes in its cuisine. Bean curd, called tofu in Japan, is extremely popular, and the Japanese can teach us much about using sea vegetables, both to flavour stocks and sauces or as a feature in the main meal. Rice is the staple commodity of the Japanese diet. Noodles form the base of some meals, and there are some appetizingly simple egg dishes.

The food of Southeast Asia provides a complete contrast to that of either China or Japan, even though most meals are based on the staple of rice. The dishes are spicy, very often made hot by the use of fresh chillies and enriched by the frequent use of coconut milk. Whereas Chinese meals are glossy combinations of carefully cut ingredients, and Japanese meals appear to be meticulously prepared and delicate, many meals from Southeast Asia are substantial mixtures of colourful ingredients prepared for families with hearty appetites. Like the meals of China and Japan, they are superbly presented, but in a more bounteous way.

One thing that all the cuisines of the East do have in common is the fact that sweet dishes are few and far between. In Southeast Asia most meals end with fresh fruit. The Japanese prefer to end with a savoury. In China the sweet-filled steamed buns and small, sweet biscuits are more often served between meals. A mixture of Oriental fruits is often the preferred dessert.

Serving Eastern Meals

As the cooking methods of each area vary, so too do the methods of serving meals. In China it is general practice to serve one main dish per person, so in a meal for four there would be four main dishes plus rice or noodles. There might also be a selection of appetizers and perhaps a soup which would not necessarily be served at the beginning of the meal. For a family meal all the dishes are placed together on the table and everyone can help themselves. If the occasion were a party or a banquet, each course would be served separately so it could be savoured or enjoyed, and a bowl of rice would always be on the table.

Chinese food is eaten from bowls, usually with chopsticks. Flat China spoons are used for soups.

In Japan each part of a meal is served separately so that its true flavours can be appreciated. Rice or noodles are served in separate bowls. The other constituents of the meal are attractively arranged on plates. Again, chopsticks are the main eating implement.

The attitude toward food in Southeast Asia is highly sociable and gregarious. There are nearly always guests at the table, and they may bring their own friends along. In consequence a wide variety of dishes, one of which has to be rice, is placed on the table at once. Food is served from and eaten off wooden platters of varying sizes. Spoons and forks can be used, but food is frequently eaten with the fingers, very often being scooped up with edible leaves. Finger bowls are never missing from the table. Etiquette varies, too. In China the first three courses of a banquet should be eaten slowly and should be accompanied by leisurely sips of Chinese rice wine or tea. This will prepare your stomach for the delights in the latter part of the feast and will ensure that you do not eat too much. Greediness is not admired in China.

In Japan each portion of the meal should be eaten at a leisurely pace. You may eat every part, but it is not necessary. In Indonesia it is polite to take third and even fourth helpings and to eat heartily. In Laos some food must always be left on the plate; otherwise you will insult your host by implying that he or she has not given you enough.

In the West choose your dishes carefully. It would be best to keep a meal to recipes from only one country. Choose the dishes well, varying colour, texture, flavour and cooking methods. We like muddled eating in the West, putting various dishes on to one plate so sauces and flavours combine together in a hazy blur. Try, just for a change, when serving Chinese or Japanese meals, to do it as the locals do and serve each part of the meal separately. You will be surprised at just how much about flavours and textures you have not noticed before.

Why not try eating a Southeast Asian meal outside on a sunny day? Sit on the floor, invite people to join you and get some idea of the happy social life of that part of the world. Equally, a variety of hot, colourful and spicy dishes can cheer the bleakest winter day.

Eastern eating can bring new moods as well as new flavours.

What to Drink with an Eastern Meal

In China no alcohol is served before a meal. While you are waiting for the food, a refreshing and fragrant China tea is served, just as it is, without milk or sugar.

Chinese wine, made from glutinous rice and not grapes, may be served throughout the meal, but for family meals a pot of tea is the most frequent accompaniment.

The Japanese also have rice wines, sake and a stronger liquor called mirin. These may be served before and during Japanese meals, and on cold days the sake may be served hot. For family meals Japanese green tea begins, accompanies and ends a meal.

In Southeast Asia the drink, as befits a hot climate, may well be beer. However, many of the people are Muslims, and for them alcohol is not allowed. Alcoholic drinks are also extremely expensive all over the area, and

9

so people mainly rely on the juice from their local fruits, which is available in great abundance and which complements the rich and spicy foods.

Some non-Muslim areas have their own varieties of rice wine, which are served on feast days.

Eastern Ingredients

If you intend to make eastern food a speciality of your kitchen, it is best to make sure that your cupboard is well stocked with the necessary spices and other flavouring ingredients. Most of these are not hard to find. If you do have difficulty, it is quite possible to use substitutes.

First of all, a word about the ingredients I have omitted altogether. Many Chinese and Japanese recipes contain rather too much sugar and also small but frequent additions of monosodium glutamate. These have simply been omitted. The dishes that should have contained them still taste good, and if you are used to eating wholefoods you will probably find them more pleasing to your palate than the original. Omitting both ingredients puts more emphasis on the natural flavours of the vegetables and other main ingredients.

Corn flour, used frequently as a thickener in Chinese dishes, is a highly refined flour. Instead use arrowroot, which is marginally more nutritious.

Herbs and Spices

CHILLIES: Chillies are used frequently in the cooking of Southeast Asia. Both red and green varieties are readily available in the West at most times of the year. Buy them from supermarkets, greengrocers and ethnic shops.

To prepare chillies, cut them in half lengthways. Cut away the core, and remove all the seeds. Wash your hands immediately after you have handled them, and do not get your hands near your eyes.

Chillies have a fresh, hot flavour. They are used in great quantity in Southeast Asian dishes. If you are not used to their flavour, cut down on the amounts by up to one half the first time you use them. If you like them you can always increase them the next time.

If no fresh chillies are available, substitute dried chillies or chilli powder. Dried chillies should be reconstituted by soaking them in hot water for 15 minutes before chopping. They are best used in stew-type dishes that have to be cooked for a long time. If you have to use chilli powder, use about one eighth of a teaspoon as a substitute for one fresh chilli.

CORIANDER: Coriander comes from the same family as parsley. The small, round, sweetly spiced seeds can be used whole or ground. The pungent fresh leaves are often chopped and used as a garnish for Chinese and Southeast Asian foods. Seeds and ground coriander can be bought in most delicatessens and ethnic shops. Fresh coriander can be bought in Chinese shops and from some markets. It can also be grown in western herb gardens.

CUMIN: Cumin seeds have a dry, spicy flavour. They are used whole or are ground in Malaysian, Ceylonese and Indian dishes.

CURRY LEAF: Curry leaves have a dry, spicy, curry-like flavour without the hotness. They are frequently used in Southeast Asian cooking and can be bought dried from some specialist shops. As a substitute use the leaves of the curry plant that is grown in some western herb gardens, or half a teaspoon mild Madras curry powder for every two leaves required.

FENUGREEK: Fenugreek is a spice that is most frequently used in curries. The small, yellow-brown, irregularly shaped seeds are frequently sold whole in wholefood shops for sprouting. They should be crushed before using them in cooked dishes.

FIVE-SPICE POWDER: Five-spice powder is used only in Chinese cooking. As its name implies it is a mixture of five ground spices: aniseed, Szechuan pepper, fennel seed, cloves and cinnamon. It can be bought from delicatessens, Chinese shops and some wholefood shops.

GINGER: Ginger root is usually used fresh in all eastern recipes. It comes in the form of a knobbly rhizome with a grey-brown skin and fibrous translucent, pale yellow flesh. Fresh ginger is widely available from greengrocers, supermarkets and specialist shops. It should be peeled before use and should be grated on a fine grater to remove the fibres. Fresh ginger has a fresh, citrus-like flavour. If it is not available, for every half ounce (15g) required use half a teaspoon ground ginger plus one tablespoon lemon or lime juice.

LEMON GRASS: Lemon grass is a herb frequently used in the cooking of Southeast Asia, where it is known as sereh. It does, in fact, look like grass and has a soft, lemony flavour. Lemon grass is becoming increasingly available in the West and can be found in some supermarkets and specialist shops. Lemon balm or lemon verbena make excellent substitutes. Failing this, add two teaspoons lemon juice for every small stalk required. This will give a slightly sharper flavour but will not be detrimental to the dish.

LAOS POWDER: Laos powder is another ingredient used frequently in Southeast Asian cookery. It is gradually becoming more readily available in the West but may be hard to find in provincial areas. Laos powder is a spice derived from a member of the ginger family; it has a somewhat peppery ginger-like flavour. If it is not available, substitute equal quantities of ground ginger and freshly ground black pepper. So for half a teaspoon Laos powder, you will need a quarter teaspoon each of ginger and pepper.

STAR-ANISE: Star-anise is a spice used in Chinese cookery. It comes in the form of a dried, star-shaped seed pod that is usually added to braised and simmered dishes to give an aniseed-like flavour. It can be bought from specialist herb and spice shops and from Chinese shops.

SZECHUAN PEPPER: Szechuan peppercorns are also featured in Chinese cookery. They are red-brown in colour and have a spicier, less hot flavour than does black pepper. They add a distinctive flavour to some dishes, but if they are not available, ordinary black peppercorns can be used instead in the same quantity.

TAMARIND: The tamarind tree grows in many tropical countries. Its fruits are dried and compressed into blocks, and small amounts are reconstituted by soaking in hot water. It is used for flavouring curries, sauces and other savoury dishes. Tamarind has a sour, fruity taste. It is widely available from delicatessens and ethnic shops, and a small block, if kept well wrapped, will last for years. However, if it is not available, use one tablespoon lemon or lime juice for each half ounce (15g) needed.

TURMERIC: Turmeric is a yellow-coloured, sweet and mildly pungent spice that is readily available in its ground form in the West. It is used in curries and spiced dishes and for flavouring and colouring rice.

Sauces and Bean Pastes

TAMARI AND SHOYU SAUCE: Soy sauce is a frequent ingredient in both Chinese and Japanese cookery and in some of the Southeast Asian recipes it has been used as a replacement for terasi, or shrimp paste, which is a common flavouring ingredient in that area. The soy sauce mostly available in western supermarkets, and frequently the Chinese varieties of soy sauce, have been produced from soya bean extract and other ingredients, including caramel. The original Japanese soy sauces are made with whole fermented soya beans. Tamari sauce is made from only soya beans and sea salt. Shoyu sauce is made from soya beans, sea salt, wheat and barley. Both have a richer flavour than the other types of soya sauce and are obviously the more wholesome products. They are also highly suitable for Chinese and Japanese dishes. Both are available from most wholefood shops and shops that specialise in Japanese food.

MISO: Miso is a paste made from fermented soya beans which is sealed in vacuum packs and which can be bought from most wholefood shops. It is featured mainly in Japanese cookery.

BEAN PASTES: Bean pastes are made by crushing or sieving yellow or black soya beans or red kidney beans and mixing them with other ingredients.

Yellow and black bean pastes are made from salted soya beans. The yellow paste has a sweet-savoury flavour. The black is drier and is often flavoured to varying degrees with chillies or chilli sauce. Yellow and black bean pastes are used in China and also in Indonesia, where they are called *tauco*. Both can be bought in cans or jars. The recipe for making black bean paste is on page 172.

Red bean paste is made from red kidney beans and sugar. There is a recipe for making your own with honey on page 172. It is used mainly in sweet recipes but can be mixed with savoury pastes for a sauce for noodles.

CHILLI SAUCE: This is made from red chillies. It is a red-orange colour and is of a consistency just a little thinner than tomato ketchup. It is very hot and may or may not be flavoured with garlic. It is mainly used in Chinese cookery.

HOISIN SAUCE: This is sometimes called Chinese barbecue sauce. It is made from soya beans and is a dark reddish-brown colour with a thick, spoonable texture and a hot and sweet flavour. It does contain sugar, but since only a small amount is used in any one dish it has been included in a few of the recipes.

TOMATO KETCHUP: It might seem surprising to find tomato ketchup in a wholefood-oriented book. However, it does make an excellent substitute for the shrimp paste used in many Southeast Asian recipes. Wherever possible, buy the sugar-free variety (produced by Whole Earth), which is available from wholefood shops.

Unusual Vegetables and Fruits

BAMBOO SHOOTS: These are rarely found fresh in the West, but excellent ones can be bought in cans, either ready-sliced or in chunks. Drain them before use.

BEAN SPROUTS: To many people who eat wholefoods, these are no longer unusual. They are produced by sprouting mung (or moong) beans. They can be bought in packets from supermarkets or loose from greengrocers, some wholefood shops and ethnic shops. You can also sprout them yourself in a jar. Bean sprouts are best used on the day of purchase (or as soon as they are ready) but will store in a polythene (plastic) bag in the refrigerator for up to two days.

DAIKON: This is also known as Japanese radish or mooli. In appearance it is like a very long, smooth, white carrot, and it has a flavour somewhere between a radish and a turnip. It can be bought from some supermarkets, from specialist greengrocers and from shops selling eastern ingredients. Daikon is most often served raw or is parboiled when used in salads.

DRIED MUSHROOMS: Special varieties of both Chinese and Japanese mushrooms are available from shops that specialize in the products of these countries. To reconstitute them soak them in hot water for twenty to thirty minutes. Then drain them. The soaking water may be kept to use in the dish instead of vegetable stock. They can be left whole, or can be halved, quartered, chopped or slivered for cooking and have a chewy texture and a pleasant, earthy flavour.

LIMES: These are readily available from greengrocers, supermarkets and ethnic shops. Lemons are not available in Southeast Asia, and limes are used in many dishes to produce a sharp but mellow citrus flavour. If they are not available, lemons may be used instead.

LOTUS ROOT: Lotus root is rarely found fresh in the West and so must be bought canned. Around the lakes where it grows it is sometimes eaten raw as a fruit, but most often it is included in a mixture of vegetables for stir-frying or is made into a salad. Canned lotus root is usually sliced. Lotus root has a pleasant, crisp texture but a slightly bland flavour. Its chief virtue seems to be its appearance. It is off-white in colour, and as the root has holes arranged in a circle running right down the length, the slices have an attractive, doilylike pattern.

Sea Vegetables

Sea vegetables provide the distinctive characteristic flavour of many Japanese dishes. They are available dried and vacuum packed from wholefood shops and shops that specialize in Japanese foods. There are three types used in this book.

KOMBU: Kombu is dried kelp. It comes in thick, dark green or grey-green sheets. It is mainly used for flavouring stocks.

BONITO: This is also called katsoubushi and comes in small, brown-yellow flakes that can be easily crumbled.

NORI: This is dried laver and comes in thin, dark green sheets which become a fresh, bright green when exposed for a short time to indirect heat.

If kombu or bonito are not available, nori can be used instead for all the recipes in this book which use sea vegetables.

Nuts and Oils

ALMONDS: These are used blanched in some Chinese stir-fried dishes and are ground to make a sweet jelly for a dessert. In Southeast Asian dishes they can be used as a substitute for macadamia nuts (see right).

CASHEW NUTS: Buy cashew nut halves or pieces from wholefood shops. They can be stir-fried with vegetables to make Chinese dishes.

COCONUT: The coconut appears frequently in Southeast Asian cooking. The actual flesh is used as well as coconut milk and coconut oil.

When buying a fresh coconut, shake it first to make sure that there is plenty of liquid inside. If there is no liquid, the flesh may well have begun to dry.

To extract the liquid first remove the 'matting' from the top of the coconut. Underneath you will find three round 'eyes'. Pierce through two of these 'eyes', using a thick skewer or a braddall (icepick). Hold the coconut over a jug to catch the liquid as it pours out.

To break a coconut put it on a hard, unbreakable surface such as concrete and smash it with a hammer. You can also simply throw it down hard on a concrete floor.

To remove the flesh use a rounded knife to score it into slices and to ease it out. Coconut can be grated on a hand grater, but it is much easier to use a grater attachment on a food processor. In theory you should cut all the brown skin away before grating. In practice, this is easier said than done, and it makes very little difference to anyone but a purist if it is included in a dish.

COCONUT OIL: is used for frying in Southeast Asia. It is a thick, white oil, which must be heated before pouring. It gives a slight coconut flavour to the dish, but it is a saturated fat and for health and ease of use groundnut (peanut) oil (see below) is to be preferred.

COCONUT MILK: Coconut milk is not the liquid inside the coconut (although this does make an extremely refreshing drink). Coconut milk is made by soaking and straining grated, fresh coconut or by using coconut cream. It is easy to make yourself from the instructions on page 19.

GROUNDNUT OIL: This is another name for peanut oil. It has been used throughout the book for sautéeing, stir-frying and deep-frying as it is particularly suitable for the dishes of all eastern countries.

MACADAMIA NUTS: Macadamia nuts are used ground in Southeast Asian cookery to thicken soups and stew-type dishes. They are small, round nuts about the size of hazelnuts and are sold free of their skins. They have a light, crumbly texture and a delicate light flavour. They can be bought in delicatessens, some wholefood shops and from shops specializing in ethnic ingredients. Blanched almonds may be used as a substitute.

PEANUTS: These appear a great deal in Southeast Asian cooking. They are very often ground to make rich sauces for vegetable dishes. Buy them shelled and unroasted.

SESAME SEEDS: Sesame seeds are used in the cooking of both China and

Japan and appear in both sweet and savoury recipes. They are now widely available from wholefood shops. The pale brown kind are the most useful.

SESAME OIL: Sesame oil is produced from sesame seeds. It has a rich, amber colour and a strong, nutty flavour. It is used in Chinese dishes to add flavour and texture at the end of cooking rather than as a frying medium.

SESAME PASTE: This is made by grinding lightly roasted sesame seeds and is sold in many wholefood shops under its middle eastern name of tahini. It is used to make sauces in both China and Japan. If possible, buy the light creamy coloured variety rather than the dark grey.

Note: All recipes serve four unless otherwise stated.
        Use either metric, imperial, or American measurements.

Chapter 1
Appetizers and Soups

At a Chinese banquet one small course will follow another until up to ten or even more different dishes have been served. At a family meal in China, all the dishes will be placed on the table at once. This also happens in Southeast Asia, but the Japanese like to savour each course separately. There are therefore no real first courses featured in any of the cuisines. However, should you wish to keep to a more western pattern for your meal, the following recipes can be served as first courses.

Tea Eggs
Soy Eggs
Chilli Eggs in Coconut Milk (half quantity for four people)
Bean Curd and Peanut Salad (half quantities)
Peanuts Toasted with Red Bean Curd Cheese (This would be more of a snack with rice wine.)
Longevity Nuts (served as above)
Tea-Simmered Chestnuts
Vinegar Rice in Seaweed Rolls
Spinach and Leek Steamed Buns
Chinese Cabbage and Black Bean Steamed Buns
Wontons
Spring Rolls
Egg Rolls
Deep-Fried Pancakes

In Chinese and Japanese cuisine, soups may be served at the beginning of the meal or as a separate course lower down on the menu. The clear soups in particular are served as palate refreshers in between rich or highly spiced dishes.

The soups of Southeast Asia are often made with coconut and are more substantial. Served with a separate bowl of rice, they could make a light meal in themselves.

VEGETABLE STOCK

Imperial (Metric)	American
1 large onion, roughly chopped	1 large onion, roughly chopped
2 large carrots, roughly chopped	2 large carrots, roughly chopped
2 celery sticks, roughly chopped	2 celery stalks, roughly chopped
1 medium potato, roughly chopped	1 medium potato, roughly chopped
4 large green cabbage leaves or curly kale or leaves of spring greens	4 large green cabbage leaves or curly kale or leaves of spring greens
Any other vegetable trimmings available	Any other vegetable trimmings available
4 tablespoons tamari or shoyu sauce	4 tablespoons tamari or shoyu sauce
2 teaspoons vegetable concentrate such as Vecon	2 tablespoons vegetable concentrate such as Vegex

1
Put all the ingredients in the largest possible saucepan, and cover with at least 6 pints (3.4 litres or 15 cups) of water.

2
Bring to a boil. Simmer, uncovered, 1 hour.

3
Cool completely, and strain.

4
Store in covered plastic containers in the refrigerator for up to 1 week, or in the freezer for up to 2 months.

KOMBU STOCK

Add 1 large sheet of the dried seaweed called kombu to other ingredients.

COCONUT MILK

Some of the Southeast Asian recipes in this and other sections call for coconut milk. Traditionally, this is made by grating a whole fresh coconut. This method makes a superior milk but, obviously, if you need the ingredient in a hurry, grating and soaking a fresh coconut is not going to be very practical. There are other, easier methods that use coconut cream or desiccated (dried) coconut.

Coconut Milk from a Fresh Coconut: Remove the coconut from its shell. Grate the flesh (it does not matter if the brown skin is included). Put the grated coconut in a bowl. Pour on a little over ¼ pint (140ml or ½ cup) hot water and let the coconut soak 20 minutes. Line a sieve with a piece of muslin. Put it over a bowl. Pour in the coconut and liquid. Bring the sides of the muslin together, and squeeze out as much liquid as possible. This makes a thick coconut milk. For a medium-thick milk add 8 fl ounces (225 ml or 1 cup water), and for a thin milk ½ pint (285 ml or 1¼ cups) water.

Coconut Milk from Desiccated (Dried) Coconut: Soak 8 ounces (225g) desiccated (dried) coconut in 1 pint (575 ml or 2¼ cups) hot water for 20 minutes. Strain and squeeze out as above. This makes only a thin milk.

Coconut milk from Coconut Cream: Put the coconut cream in a bowl, and pour on very hot water. Stir well so the coconut cream dissolves. Strain through a nylon sieve, and add a pinch of sea salt as this milk tends to be sweet.

For thick coconut milk use 4 ounces (115 g or ½ cup) to ½ pint (285 ml or 1¼ cups) water; for medium, 3 ounces (85 g or ⅓ cup); and for thin 2 ounces (50g or ¼ cup).

The Easy Way: Coconut milk can be bought in tins from delicatessens and shops that specialize in eastern food. It is usually thick and needs to be thinned before using. To make it medium-thick add 3 fl ounces (90ml or ⅓ cup) water per every ¼ pint (140 ml or ⅔ cup); for thin, add 4 fl ounces (125 ml or ½ cup) water.

CELESTIAL SOUP

China

This soup is served between meals to refresh the palate. It is also called The Soup of the Gods. It is the simplest of all the Chinese soups, but the flavour is nonetheless delicious. The beaten egg is optional, but it does make the soup more substantial should you wish to serve it at the beginning of the meal.

Imperial (Metric)	American
1¼ pints (850ml) vegetable stock	3¾ cups vegetable stock
2 tablespoons tamari or shoyu sauce	2 tablespoons tamari or shoyu sauce
Pinch of sea salt and freshly ground pepper if needed	Pinch of sea salt and freshly ground pepper if needed
1 egg, beaten	1 egg, beaten
2 spring onions, finely chopped	2 scallions, finely chopped
1 teaspoon sesame oil	1 teaspoon sesame oil

1
Bring the stock to a boil. Add the tamari or shoyu sauce, and season if wished.

2
Slowly pour in the egg over the prongs of a fork. Beat it so it sets in thin shreds.

3
Pour the soup into a warmed tureen.

4
Sprinkle the spring onions (scallions) and sesame oil over the top.

Note: Traditionally, the bowl is placed in the centre of the table and guests can help themselves to the soup between courses. The soup can be frozen without the egg or garnishes. Cool it completely, and store it for up to 2 months in rigid, sealed plastic containers. Thaw at room temperature.

MUSHROOM AND GREEN PEA SOUP

China

Imperial (Metric)	American
6 Chinese mushrooms	6 Chinese mushrooms
½ pint (285ml) boiling water	1¼ cups boiling water
4 ounces (115g) bean curd	¼ pound bean curd
Up to 1½ pints (850ml) vegetable stock	Up to 3¾ cups vegetable stock
2 tablespoons tamari or shoyu sauce	2 tablespoons tamari or shoyu sauce
2 tablespoons Chinese rice wine or dry sherry	2 tablespoons Chinese rice wine or dry sherry
8 ounces (225g) shelled green peas	1⅓ cups shelled green peas

1

Put the mushrooms in a bowl, and pour on the boiling water. Let soak 30 minutes. Drain the mushrooms, reserving the water. Finely chop them. Increase the water up to 1½ pints (850ml or 3¾ cups) with the stock.

2

Finely chop the bean curd.

3

Put the stock into a saucepan, and bring it to a boil. Add the tamari or shoyu sauce, rice wine or sherry and mushrooms. Cover and simmer 10 minutes.

4

Add the peas and simmer, uncovered, 8 minutes.

5

Add the bean curd, and cook 2 minutes more.

Note: Not suitable for freezing.

WATERCRESS SOUP

China

Imperial (Metric)	American
4 ounces (115g) watercress	2 cups watercress, chopped
1½ pints (850ml) vegetable stock	3¾ cups vegetable stock
2 tablespoons tamari or shoyu sauce	2 tablespoons tamari or shoyu sauce
4 tablespoons Chinese rice wine or dry sherry	4 tablespoons Chinese rice wine or dry sherry
½ teaspoon sea salt	½ teaspoon sea salt
Freshly ground black pepper	Freshly ground black pepper
2 eggs, beaten	2 eggs, beaten
4 spring onions, finely chopped	4 scallions, finely chopped
2 teaspoons sesame oil	2 teaspoons sesame oil

1

Finely chop the watercress.

2

Put the stock in a saucepan. Bring it to a boil. Add the tamari or shoyu sauce, wine or sherry and seasonings.

3

Turn down the heat. Briefly take the pan from the heat to let the stock come to just below boiling point. Put it back on the heat. Pour in the eggs over the prongs of a fork in a thin stream. Stir.

4

Add the watercress, and bring the soup back to a boil.

5

Pour the soup into four individual bowls. Sprinkle it with sesame oil and spring onions (scallions) just before serving.

Note: Not suitable for freezing.

SWEETCORN AND EGG SOUP

China

Imperial (Metric)	American
One 12 oz (340g) tin sweetcorn	1½ cups sweetcorn
1 tablespoon arrowroot	1 tablespoon arrowroot
1½ pints (850ml) vegetable stock	3¾ cups vegetable stock
1 tablespoon sesame oil	1 tablespoon sesame oil
1 teaspoon ground ginger	1 teaspoon ground ginger
1 tablespoon tamari or shoyu sauce	1 tablespoon tamari or shoyu sauce
2 tablespoons Chinese rice wine or dry sherry	2 tablespoons Chinese rice wine or dry sherry
2 eggs, beaten	2 eggs, beaten
2 spring onions, finely chopped	2 scallions, finely chopped

1

Put the sweetcorn in a blender or food processor with the arrowroot. Blend until the sweetcorn is well broken up but has not been reduced to a smooth purée.

2

Put the stock in a saucepan, and bring it to a boil. Add the sesame oil and ground ginger, and simmer 2 minutes.

3

Add the sweetcorn, tamari or shoyu sauce and wine or sherry. Bring to just below boiling point, stirring.

4

Pour in the eggs over the prongs of a fork in a thin stream. Stir well so they set in shreds.

5

Pour the soup into individual bowls, and scatter the spring onions (scallions) over the top.

Note: Not suitable for freezing.

TOMATO AND EGG FLOWER SOUP

China

Imperial (Metric)	American
1 pound (455g) tomatoes	1 pound tomatoes
2 medium onions	2 medium onions
3 tablespoons groundnut oil	3 tablespoons peanut oil
1½ pints (850ml) vegetable stock	3¾ cups vegetable stock
2 tablespoons Chinese rice wine or dry sherry	2 tablespoons Chinese rice wine or dry sherry
2 teaspoons tamari or shoyu sauce	2 teaspoons tamari or shoyu sauce
2 eggs, beaten	2 eggs, beaten

1

Cut each tomato into eight lengthways slices. Halve the onions lengthways. Cut them into thin, crescent-shaped pieces.

2

Heat the oil in a saucepan over low heat. Put in the onions, and soften them. Put in the tomatoes, and cook, stirring frequently, 2 minutes.

3

Pour in the stock, and bring it to a boil. Add the wine or sherry and tamari or shoyu sauce.

4

Pour in the eggs over the prongs of a fork in a thin stream. Stir until set.

Note: Not suitable for freezing.

SPINACH AND BEAN CURD SOUP

China

Imperial (Metric)	American
8 ounces (225g) spinach	2 cups spinach
10 ounces (285g) bean curd	1¼ pound bean curd
4 spring onions	4 scallions
1½ pints (850ml) stock	3¾ cups stock
2 tablespoons tamari or shoyu sauce	2 tablespoons tamari or shoyu sauce

1
Wash the spinach, trim away the stalks, and roughly chop the leaves. Cut the bean curd into ⅜ inch (1 cm) cubes. Finely chop the spring onions (scallions).

2
Bring the stock to a boil. Put in the tamari sauce, spinach, bean curd and spring onions (scallions). Simmer 5 minutes.

3
Serve as soon as possible so that the spinach retains its bright green colour.

Note: Not suitable for freezing.

HOT AND SOUR SOUP

China

Imperial (Metric)	American
4 Chinese dried mushrooms	4 Chinese dried mushrooms
10 ounces (285g) bean curd	1¼ pounds bean curd
4 spring onions	4 scallions
2 ounces (55g) bamboo shoots	½ cup bamboo shoots
1 tablespoon arrowroot	1 tablespoon arrowroot
¼ teaspoon freshly ground black pepper	¼ teaspoon freshly ground black pepper
2 tablespoons tamari or shoyu sauce	2 tablespoons tamari or shoyu sauce
2 tablespoons white wine vinegar	2 tablespoons white wine vinegar
1½ pints (850ml) vegetable stock	3¾ cups vegetable stock
½ ounce (15g) ginger root, peeled and grated	½ ounce fresh ginger, peeled and grated
2 tablespoons Szechuan pickled vegetables (optional)	2 tablespoons Szechuan pickled vegetables (optional)
2 eggs, beaten	2 eggs, beaten

1

Soak the mushrooms in hot water 30 minutes. Drain them, and cut them into thin shreds. Finely chop the bean curd and the spring onions (scallions). Cut the bamboo shoots into thin shreds.

2

Put the arrowroot in a bowl. Add the pepper. Gradually mix in the tamari or shoyu sauce, vinegar and 4 tablespoons of the stock.

3

Put the remaining stock in a saucepan and bring it to a boil. Put in the mushrooms, cover and simmer 5 minutes.

Note: Not suitable for freezing.

CHINESE CABBAGE AND TRANSPARENT NOODLE SOUP

China

Imperial (Metric)	American
8 dried Chinese mushrooms	8 dried Chinese mushrooms
4 ounces (115g) transparent noodles	¼ pound transparent noodles
2½ pounds (1.275 kilos) Chinese cabbage	2¼ pounds Chinese cabbage
2 tablespoons groundnut oil	2 tablespoons peanut oil
1½ pints (850ml) vegetable stock	3¾ cups vegetable stock
2 tablespoons tamari or shoyu sauce	2 tablespoons tamari or shoyu sauce
2 tablespoons red wine vinegar	2 tablespoons red wine vinegar
2 spring onions, finely chopped	2 scallions, finely chopped
1¼ teaspoons sesame oil	1¼ teaspoons sesame oil

1

Soak the mushrooms in boiling water 30 minutes. Drain, and cut into thin strips. Soak the noodles in hot water 5 minutes. Drain. Cut the cabbage into 1-inch (2.5cm) pieces.

2

Heat the oil in a large saucepan over high heat. Put in the mushrooms and cabbage, and stir-fry 3 minutes.

3

Pour in the stock, and bring it to a boil. Add the tamari or shoyu sauce and vinegar, and simmer 5 minutes.

4

Add the noodles. Bring the soup back to a boil. Cover and simmer 20 minutes.

5

Add the spring onions (scallions) and sesame oil. Simmer, uncovered, 2 minutes. Serve as soon as possible.

Note: Not suitable for freezing.

SIZZLING RICE SOUP

China

Imperial (Metric)	American
4 ounces (115g) open mushrooms	2 cups mushrooms
2 ounces (55g) bamboo shoots	¼ cup bamboo shoots
2 ounces (55g) drained, tinned water chestnuts	¼ cup drained, canned water chestnuts
1½ pints (850ml) vegetable stock	3¾ cups vegetable stock
2 tablespoons tamari or shoyu sauce	2 tablespoons tamari or shoyu sauce
2 tablespoons Chinese rice wine or dry sherry	2 tablespoons Chinese rice wine or dry sherry
4 ounces (115g) shelled peas	⅔ cup shelled peas
Eight 2-inch (5 cm) squares crisp rice (page 125)	Eight 2-inch squares crisp rice (page 125)
Oil for deep-frying	Oil for deep-frying

1

Quarter the mushrooms. Thinly slice the bamboo shoots and water chestnuts.

2

Bring the stock to a boil. Add the tamari or shoyu sauce and wine or sherry. Then put in the mushrooms, bamboo shoots, water chestnuts and peas. Simmer, uncovered, 10 minutes.

3

Heat the oil to a temperature of 350F/180C. Deep-fry the pieces of crisp rice, two at a time, until golden brown, about 1 minute. Lift them out, and drain on paper towels.

4

Put the pieces of rice in a large tureen. Pour the soup over them. They should crackle and sizzle.

Note: The soup can be frozen before it is poured over the rice. Cool it completely. Put it into a rigid plastic container and cover. Store for up to two months. Thaw at room temperature, and reheat in a saucepan.

JAPANESE MISO SOUP

Japan

Imperial (Metric)	American
1¼ pints (850ml) kombu stock	3¾ cups kombu stock
3 ounces (85g) miso (soya bean paste)	⅓ cup miso (soybean paste)

1

Put the stock in a saucepan. Place a sieve over the pan. Put the miso into the sieve, and rub it through, moistening it with the stock as and when necessary.

2

Bring the soup to simmering point over medium heat.

3

Take the pan from the heat.

4

Pour the soup into bowls. Stir each one, and garnish.

Garnishes for Miso Soup

Use one or more of the following:

Chopped spring onions (scallions)

Japanese white radish (also called monli or diakon) cut into thin strips, blanched for 2 minutes and drained.

Wakame (another type of dried seaweed) soaked in warm water for 15 minutes, chopped and simmered for 1 minute in the soup.

Bean curd (about 6 oz (170g) chopped and simmered in the soup for 1 minute.

Note: Not suitable for freezing.

CURRIED VEGETABLE SOUP

Indonesia

Imperial (Metric)	American
½ teaspoon ground turmeric	½ teaspoon ground turmeric
¼ teaspoon Laos powder (or pinch each ground ginger and freshly ground black pepper)	¼ teaspoon Laos powder (or pinch each ground ginger and freshly ground black pepper)
1 garlic clove, finely chopped	1 garlic clove, finely chopped
1 medium onion, finely chopped	1 medium onion, finely chopped
2 tablespoons groundnut oil	2 tablespoons peanut oil
8 ounces (225g) potato	1 medium potato
8 ounces (225g) carrots	1 to 2 carrots
4 ounces (115g) green cabbage	1 cup green cabbage
1 green pepper	1 green pepper
4 ounces (115g) shelled green peas	⅔ cup shelled green peas
¾ pint (425ml) medium-thick coconut milk	2 cups medium-thick coconut milk
¾ pint (425ml) vegetable stock	2 cups vegetable stock
2 curry leaves, chopped	2 curry leaves, chopped
1 stalk lemon grass, chopped	1 stalk lemon grass, chopped

1

Put the turmeric, Laos powder, garlic, onion and 1 tablespoon oil in a blender or food processor. Work to a smooth paste.

2

Peel and chop the potatoes. Thinly slice the carrots. Shred the cabbage. Core and seed the pepper, and chop it.

3

Heat the remaining oil in a wok or large shallow pan over a medium heat. Put in the spice and onion paste. Stir-fry 2 minutes, or until it gives off a delicious aromatic scent and no longer sticks to the sides of the pan.

4

Add the coconut milk and stock, and bring them to a boil. Add the vegetables, curry leaves and lemon grass. Simmer, uncovered, until the vegetables are just tender, about 20 minutes.

Note: To freeze, cool completely. Pour into a rigid plastic container and seal. Store for up to two months. Thaw at room temperature, and reheat gently.

THICK, GREEN VEGETABLE SOUP

Indonesia

Imperial (Metric)	American
1 pound (455g) spring greens or spinach or green cabbage	1 pound collards or spinach or green cabbage
4 macadamia nuts or blanched almonds	4 macadamia nuts or blanched almonds
1 teaspoon coriander seeds	1 teaspoon coriander seeds
1 medium onion, finely chopped	1 medium onion, finely chopped
1 garlic clove, finely chopped	1 garlic clove, finely chopped
2 tablespoons water	2 tablespoons water
1¼ pints (710ml) medium-thick coconut milk	3 cups medium-thick coconut milk
½ teaspoon Laos powder, or ¼ teaspoon each ground ginger and freshly ground black pepper	½ teaspoon Laos powder, or ¼ teaspoon each ground ginger and freshly ground black pepper
2 curry leaves	2 curry leaves

1

Finely chop the spinach, greens or cabbage.

2

Put the nuts and coriander seeds in a blender or food processor. Grind finely. Add the onion, garlic, and water and work the ingredients to a paste.

3

Put the coconut milk in a saucepan with the Laos powder and curry leaves, and bring it to a boil. Add the almond and coriander paste, and stir. Simmer, uncovered, 2 minutes.

4

Add the green vegetables and simmer, uncovered — spinach 3 minutes, spring greens (collards) 10 minutes, cabbage 5 to 7 minutes or until just tender.

Note: Not suitable for freezing.

PUMPKIN AND COCONUT MILK SOUP

Laos

Imperial (Metric)	American
3 pounds (1.35kilos) pumpkin	3 pounds pumpkin
12 fl ounces (340ml) coconut milk	1½ cups coconut milk
3 small shallots or 1 medium onion, finely chopped	3 small shallots or 1 medium onion, finely chopped
2 tablespoons chopped, fresh coriander	2 tablespoons chopped, fresh coriander
Pinch of sea salt	Pinch of sea salt
2 tablespoons tamari or shoyu sauce	2 tablespoons tamari or shoyu sauce
Freshly ground black pepper	Freshly ground black pepper
4 spring onions, finely chopped	4 scallions, finely chopped

1

Remove the peel and seeds from the pumpkin. Finely chop the flesh.

2

Put it in a saucepan with the coconut milk, shallots or onion, coriander and sea salt.

3

Bring everything to a boil over medium heat. Add the tamari or shoyu sauce. Cover and simmer until the pumpkin is very soft and can be mashed to a purée, about 30 minutes. Season to taste with the pepper.

4

Pour the soup into four individual bowls, and scatter the spring onions (scallions) over the top.

Note: To freeze, cool the soup completely. Pour it into a rigid plastic container and seal tightly. Store in the freezer for up to two months. Thaw at room temperature, and reheat gently.

Chapter 2
Egg Dishes

Eggs are used a great deal in Chinese cookery and dishes made from them vary from the very simple, delicately flavoured Tea Eggs and Soy Eggs to more complicated stir-fried dishes and the Fu Yung, which although in Chinese restaurants in the West is more like a take-away omelette, is in actual fact a very delicately flavoured dish made only from the white.

In Southeast Asia eggs are mostly cooked with hot spices and with curry flavours. They vary in texture from the light Chilli Omelettes to the substantial Dhall Egg Curry with Lentils.

The Japanese have few egg dishes, but the chilled egg custard (page 48) stands out for its simplicity and subtle flavour.

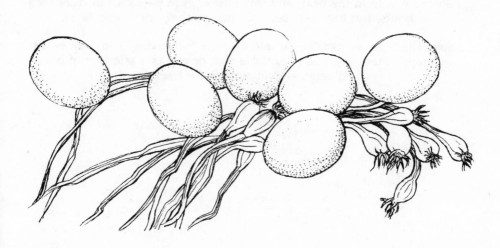

SOY EGGS

China

Imperial (Metric)	American
8 eggs	8 eggs
7 fl ounces (200ml) tamari or shoyu sauce	¾ cup tamari or shoyu sauce
3 fl ounces (90ml) water	⅓ cup water
1 teaspoon dark Barbados sugar	1 teaspoon dark brown sugar
¼ teaspoon sea salt	¼ teaspoon sea salt
2 tablespoons sesame oil	2 tablespoons sesame oil

1

Boil the eggs for 5 minutes. Drain, and pour cold water over them. Leave 5 minutes. Drain again, and shell.

2

In a saucepan, mix together the remaining ingredients. Bring the mixture to simmering point, and carefully put in the eggs. Leave the eggs over very low heat 2 minutes, turning them after 1 minute.

3

Take the pan from the heat, and leave the eggs in the sauce mixture for 4 hours, turning them several times so they colour evenly.

Note: The eggs are usually cut into quarters for serving. They can be an accompaniment to a main vegetable dish or part of a selection of hors d'oeuvres. Not suitable for freezing.

TEA EGGS

China

Imperial (Metric)	American
8 eggs	8 eggs
1 teaspoon sea salt	1 teaspoon sea salt
1 whole star anise	1 whole star anise
3 tablespoons tamari or shoyu sauce	3 tablespoons tamari or shoyu sauce
1 tablespoon China tea leaves	1 tablespoon China tea leaves

1

Hard boil the eggs for 10 minutes. Drain, and cool slightly. Tap the eggs all over with the back of a teaspoon, making a network of cracks all over them.

2

Return the eggs to the saucepan. Cover with fresh water. Add the remaining ingredients. Bring the eggs to a boil. Cover and simmer 1 hour. Cool the eggs in the liquid for 2 hours.

3

Peel the eggs just before serving. They should be patterned with a brown marbling.

Note: Serve as an appetizer or as one of the many small courses included in a Chinese banquet. Not suitable for freezing.

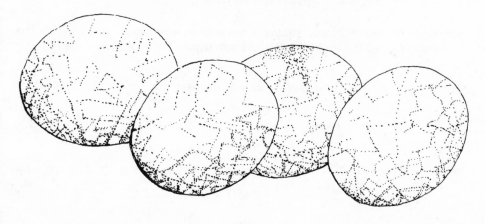

COIN PURSE EGGS

China

Imperial (Metric)	American
8 eggs	8 eggs
3 fl ounces (90ml) groundnut oil	⅓ cup peanut oil
Sea salt and freshly ground black pepper	Sea salt and freshly ground black pepper
4 tablespoons tamari or shoyu sauce	4 tablespoons tamari or shoyu sauce
2 tablespoons white wine vinegar	2 tablespoons white wine vinegar
4 tablespoons chopped, fresh coriander or parsley	4 tablespoons chopped, fresh coriander or parsley

1

Heat 2 tablespoons of the oil in a frying pan over moderate heat. Break in one egg, if possible getting the yolk to one side. Season to taste, and fry until the underside is set. Fold over one side of the white to cover the yolk completely. Turn up the heat. Cook until the underside is brown. Turn the egg over, and brown the other side.

2

Cook the remaining eggs in the same way.

3

Arrange them on a warmed serving plate.

4

Mix together the tamari or shoyu sauce and wine vinegar, and sprinkle the mixture over the eggs. Scatter the coriander or parsley over the top.

Note: Not suitable for freezing.

STIR-FRIED EGGS AND SPINACH

China

Imperial (Metric)	American
6 eggs	6 eggs
4 tablespoons tamari or shoyu sauce	4 tablespoons tamari or shoyu sauce
4 spring onions, finely chopped	4 scallions, finely chopped
12 ounces (340g) spinach	3 cups spinach
3 fl ounces (90ml) groundnut or sunflower oil	⅓ cup peanut or sunflower oil
½ tablespoon hoisin sauce	½ tablespoon hoisin sauce
2 tablespoons Chinese rice wine or dry sherry	2 tablespoons Chinese rice wine or dry sherry
Hot Black Bean and Tomato Sauce for serving (page 178)	Hot Black Bean and Tomato Sauce for serving (page 178)

1

Beat the eggs with 2 tablespoons tamari or shoyu sauce and the spring onions (scallions). Wash the spinach, and drain it well. Break off the stems where they join the leaves. Chop the leaves.

2

Heat three tablespoons of the oil in a wok or large frying pan over high heat. Pour in the egg mixture. Cook it, tipping the pan and lifting the sides of the setting egg, until it is almost set. Take the pan from the heat.

3

In a second pan, heat the remaining oil over high heat. Put in the spinach, and stir-fry 3 minutes, or until it is beginning to wilt. Add the remaining tamari or shoyu sauce and the hoisin sauce. Stir-fry 1 minute more.

4

Tip the egg into the spinach. Stir it round to break it up, and mix it with the spinach. Add the rice wine or sherry. Stir again and remove the pan from the heat.

5

Serve the Hot Black Bean and Tomato Sauce separately.

Note: Not suitable for freezing.

EGG POUCH OMELETTES

China

Imperial (Metric)	American
3 eggs	3 eggs
6 ounces (170g) leeks, very finely chopped	1 medium leek, very finely chopped
2 tablespoons tamari or shoyu sauce	2 tablespoons tamari or shoyu sauce
Pinch of ground ginger	Pinch of ground ginger
Freshly ground black pepper	Freshly ground black pepper
2 tablespoons groundnut oil	2 tablespoons peanut oil
2 tablespoons chopped, fresh coriander or parsley	2 tablespoons chopped, fresh coriander or parsley
Sauce:	Sauce:
1½ tablespoons arrowroot	1½ tablespoons arrowroot
4 fl ounces (125ml) vegetable stock	½ cup vegetable stock
1 tablespoon tamari or shoyu sauce	1 tablespoon tamari or shoyu sauce
1 tablespoon hoisin sauce	1 tablespoon hoisin sauce

1

Beat the eggs together. Mix together the leeks, tamari or shoyu sauce, ginger and pepper.

2

Heat the oil in a frying pan or wok over low heat. Put in 1 tablespoon of the beaten egg, and spread it out to make a tiny omelette. When the underside has set, put a small portion of the leek mixture on to one side of the omelette. Fold over the other side, and transfer the omelette to a plate.

3

Cook the rest in the same way.

4

Put the omelettes in a steamer, and set over boiling water. Cover and steam 25 minutes.

5

To make the sauce, mix the arrowroot with 2 tablespoons of the stock.
Bring the remaining stock to a boil in a saucepan. Stir in the tamari or
shoyu sauce and hoisin sauce. Pour in the arrowroot mixture. Stir until the
sauce thickens, and take the pan from the heat.

6

Put the cooked omelettes on a warm serving plate. Spoon the sauce over
the top, and sprinkle on the coriander or parsley.

Note: Not suitable for freezing.

STIR-FRIED EGGS AND PEAS

China

Imperial (Metric)	American
6 eggs	6 eggs
4 tablespoons tamari or shoyu sauce	4 tablespoons tamari or shoyu sauce
4 spring onions, finely chopped	4 scallions, finely chopped
5 tablespoons groundnut or sunflower oil	5 tablespoons peanut or sunflower oil
8 ounces (225g) cooked green peas	½ cup cooked green peas
½ tablespoon hoisin sauce	½ tablespoon hoisin sauce
2 tablespoons Chinese rice wine or dry sherry	2 tablespoons Chinese rice wine or dry sherry
Sweet and Sour Sauce for serving (page 173)	Sweet and Sour Sauce for serving (page 173)

1

Beat the eggs with 2 tablespoons tamari or shoyu sauce and the spring onions (scallions).

2

Heat 3 tablespoons of the oil in a wok or large frying pan over high heat. Pour in the egg mixture. Cook, tipping the sides of the pan and lifting the setting egg, until almost set. Take the pan from the heat.

3

In a second pan, heat the remaining oil over high heat. Put in the peas. Add the remaining tamari or shoyu sauce and the hoisin sauce. Stir-fry 1 minute.

4

Tip the egg into the peas and stir it round to break it up. Add the rice wine or sherry, and stir again. Take the pan from the heat.

Note: Not suitable for freezing.

FRENCH BEANS FU YUNG

China

Imperial (Metric)	American
1 pound (450g) French beans	1 pound French beans
2 tablespoons tamari or shoyu sauce	2 tablespoons tamari or shoyu sauce
4 egg whites	4 egg whites
Pinch of fine sea salt	Pinch of fine sea salt
1 tablespoon arrowroot	1 tablespoon arrowroot
3 tablespoons single cream or top of the milk	3 tablespoons light cream or half and half
3 fl ounces (90ml) groundnut oil	⅓ cup peanut oil

1

Top and tail the beans. Break into 1-inch (2.5cm) lengths. Cook in boiling water 3 minutes. Drain. Tip them into a bowl, and mix in the tamari or shoyu sauce.

2

Beat the egg white with the sea salt and arrowroot until it just begins to stiffen. Beat in the cream.

3

Heat 2 tablespoons of the oil in a large frying pan or wok over high heat. Put in the French beans with the sauce, and stir-fry 2 minutes. Remove.

4

Put the remaining oil in the pan. Reduce the heat to medium. Add the beaten egg white, and turn it in the oil until it sets.

5

Add the French beans to the pan. Mix into the egg whites, and cook 1 minute.

Note: Not suitable for freezing.

YELLOW FLOWING EGG

China

Imperial (Metric)	American
4 Chinese dried mushrooms	4 Chinese dried mushrooms
5 eggs	5 eggs
Pinch of sea salt	Pinch of sea salt
Freshly ground black pepper	Freshly ground black pepper
1 tablespoon arrowroot	1 tablespoon arrowroot
¼ pint (140ml) vegetable stock	⅔ cup vegetable stock
8 ounces (225g) bean curd	½ pound bean curd
4 tablespoons groundnut oil	4 tablespoons peanut oil
1 garlic clove, crushed	1 garlic clove, crushed
3 ounces (85g) cooked green peas	½ cup cooked green peas
1½ tablespoons sesame oil	1½ tablespoons sesame oil
2 tablespoons Chinese rice wine	2 tablespoons Chinese rice wine
or dry sherry	or dry sherry

1

Soak the mushrooms in hot water for 30 minutes. Drain, and cut each one into eight tiny wedge-shaped pieces.

2

Beat the eggs well with the salt, pepper, arrowroot and stock so you have a well-blended, smooth mixture.

3

Chop and mash the bean curd.

4

Heat half the oil in a wok or large frying pan over medium heat. Pour in the egg mixture, and stir it with a wooden spoon until it is thick, about 5 minutes. Take the pan from the heat.

5

Heat the remaining oil in a small saucepan over high heat. Add the garlic and mushrooms and stir-fry 1 minute. Add the peas, and cook for a further 30 seconds.

6

Add the bean curd and sesame oil, and stir 2 minutes. Take the pan from the heat.

7

Tip the contents of the pan into the egg, mix well, and mix in the wine or sherry.

Note: This will be quite liquid and should be served poured over rice. Not suitable for freezing.

EGGS WITH STIR-FRIED SAUCE

China

Imperial (Metric)	American
3 dried Chinese mushrooms	3 dried Chinese mushrooms
1 Chinese cabbage	1 Chinese cabbage
4 celery sticks	4 celery stalks
5 ounces (140g) drained, tinned bamboo shoots	1 cup drained, canned bamboo shoots
2 teaspoons arrowroot	2 teaspoons arrowroot
1 tablespoon tamari or shoyu sauce	1 tablespoon tamari or shoyu sauce
1 tablespoon Chinese rice wine or dry sherry	1 tablespoon Chinese rice wine or dry sherry
¼ pint (140ml) vegetable stock	⅔ cup vegetable stock
2 tablespoons groundnut oil	2 tablespoons peanut oil
1 garlic clove, crushed	1 garlic clove, crushed
8 eggs	8 eggs
Groundnut oil for frying	Peanut oil for frying

1

Soak the mushrooms in hot water 30 minutes. Drain, and thinly slice.

2

Finely shred 4 oz (115g or ¼ pound) of the cabbage. Arrange a bed of the remaining leaves on each of four dinner plates. (You may not wish to use all you have left if it is a large cabbage.)

3

Cut the celery sticks into diagonal slices from top to bottom. Thinly slice the bamboo shoots.

4

Put the arrowroot in a bowl, and mix in the tamari or shoyu sauce, rice wine or sherry and stock.

5

Heat the 2 tablespoons oil in a wok or large frying pan. Put in the garlic, mushrooms, Chinese cabbage and bamboo shoots. Stir-fry 3 minutes.

6

Give the arrowroot mixture a stir, and pour it into the pan. Cook, stirring, a further 3 minutes so vegetables are in a small amount of thick sauce. Take the pan from the heat, but keep the vegetables warm.

7

In a small wok or saucepan, heat about 1 inch (2.5cm) of oil over high heat. Drop in the eggs one at a time, and cook until set.

8

Lift out the eggs with a perforated spoon, letting them drain as much as possible. Put them directly on to the waiting beds of Chinese cabbage.

9

When all the eggs are done, spoon the stir-fried vegetables over the top.

Note: Not suitable for freezing.

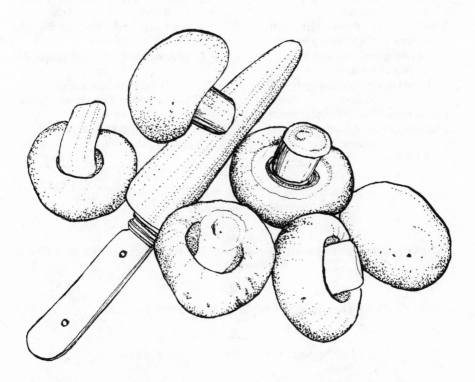

EGG TOPPED VEGETABLES WITH PANCAKES

China

Imperial (Metric)	American
4 eggs	4 eggs
2 ounces (55g) transparent noodles	2 ounces transparent noodles
8 ounces (225g) Chinese cabbage	½ pound Chinese cabbage
4 ounces (115g) drained, tinned bamboo shoots	¾ cup drained, canned bamboo shoots
Up to 4 fl ounces (125ml) groundnut oil	Up to ½ cup peanut oil
3 tablespoons tamari or shoyu sauce	3 tablespoons tamari or shoyu sauce
1 garlic clove, finely chopped	1 garlic clove, finely chopped
8 ounces (225g) bean sprouts	4 cups bean sprouts
6 spring onions, cut into matchstick pieces	6 scallions, cut into matchstick pieces
16 Mandarin pancakes (page 00)	16 Mandarin pancakes (page 00)
Sauce:	Sauce:
3 fl ounces (90ml) hoisin sauce	⅓ cup hoisin sauce
2 tablespoons tamari or shoyu sauce	2 tablespoons tamari or shoyu sauce
1 tablespoon sesame oil	1 tablespoon sesame oil

1

Beat each egg separately.

2

Soak the noodles in hot water 5 minutes. Drain, and cut into 2-inch (10cm) lengths.

3

Finely shred the cabbage and bamboo shoots.

4

Mix the ingredients for the sauce together.

5

Heat 4 tablespoons of the oil in a wok or large frying pan over high heat. Add 2 tablespoons tamari or shoyu sauce and garlic, and mix in the Chinese cabbage, bamboo shoots and bean sprouts. Stir-fry 4 minutes. Remove the vegetables. Put them in a bowl, and keep warm.

6

Set the pan back on the heat. Add 1 tablespoon more oil and the remaining tamari or shoyu sauce. Put in the noodles, and stir-fry 1 minute. Mix them into the vegetables.

7

Heat 1 tablespoon of the remaining oil in a small frying pan or wok over medium heat. Pour in one of the eggs, and tip the pan to spread it out into a thin omelette. When the underside is just turning colour, turn the omelette over. Cook the remaining eggs in the same way, adding more oil to the pan as and when necessary.

8

Divide the vegetable and noodle mixture among four dinner plates. Place an omelette on top of each portion.

9

To serve, have the sauce and the spring onions (scallions) in separate small bowls. Ideally, each person should have his or her own bowl, but slightly larger bowls may be placed in the centre of the table. Each person tears off a piece of egg and puts it into a pancake together with some of the vegetables, sauce and a sprinkling of onion. The pancakes are eaten with the fingers.

Note: Not suitable for freezing.

JAPANESE EGG CUSTARD

Japan

Imperial (Metric)	American
6 eggs	6 eggs
¾ pint (425ml) kombu stock (page 18)	2 cups kombu stock (page 18)
Pinch of sea salt	Pinch of sea salt
Grated rind of 1 lime	Grated rind of 1 lime
Sauce:	Sauce:
2 tablespoons tamari or shoyu sauce	2 tablespoons tamari or shoyu sauce
2 tablespoons sake or dry sherry	2 tablespoons sake or dry sherry
¼ pint (140ml) kombu stock	⅔ cup kombu stock
3 tablespoons flaked, dried bonito or kombu that has been torn into tiny pieces	3 tablespoons flaked, dried bonito or kombu that has been torn into tiny pieces

1

Make the sauce by putting all the sauce ingredients in a saucepan, bringing to a boil, and cooling to room temperature.

2

Beat the eggs in a bowl. Beat in the stock and sea salt.

3

Line a 1½ pint (850ml or 3¾ cup), 2-inch (5 cm) deep, round baking tin with aluminium foil. Pour in the egg mixture. Cover with more foil. Place the tin in a large steamer.

4

Lower the steamer over a pan of boiling water. Cover and steam over moderate heat 4 minutes. Turn heat to simmer. Slightly open the steamer lid, and continue cooking for 20 minutes or until the eggs are set.

5

Run a knife around the edge of the custard. Cut the custard into 4 pieces. Dip the bottom of the tin into ice-cold water. Place a flat plate on top of the tin and turn out the custard. Wrap each piece of custard in cling film (plastic wrap) and put them in the refrigerator to chill for 30 minutes.

6

Strain the sauce, and divide it among four dishes. Put the pieces of custard on a serving plate and scatter the lime rind over the top. Serve the sauce separately.

Note: Not suitable for freezing.

DHALL EGG CURRY

Malaysia

Imperial (Metric)	American
8 ounces (225g) split, red lentils	1 cup split, red lentils
4 eggs, hard boiled	4 hard-boiled eggs
2 ounces (50g) ghee or butter	4 tablespoons ghee or butter
2 medium onions, finely chopped	2 medium onions, finely chopped
1½ tablespoons curry powder	1½ tablespoons curry powder

1

Soak the lentils in cold water for 8 hours or overnight. Drain.

2

Peel and halve the eggs.

3

Heat the ghee or butter in a saucepan over low heat. Put in the onions, and cook, stirring frequently, until brown.

4

Add the lentils and curry powder. Cook 5 minutes, stirring.

5

Pour in ½ pint (245ml or 1⅓ cups) hot water. Simmer, covered, about 20 minutes, or until the lentils are tender and all the liquid has been absorbed.

6

Put in the egg halves, and cook 2 minutes more.

Note: Not suitable for freezing.

CHILLI OMELETTES

Indonesia

Imperial (Metric)	American
8 eggs	8 eggs
3 tablespoons water	3 tablespoons water
4 teaspoons tamari or shoyu sauce	4 teaspoons tamari or shoyu sauce
4 red or green chillies	4 red or green chilis
4 tablespoons groundnut oil	4 tablespoons peanut oil
1 medium onion, finely chopped	1 medium onion, finely chopped

1

Beat the eggs, four at a time, each four with half the water and half the tamari or shoyu sauce.

2

Halve the chillies lengthways. Core and seed them, and cut into very thin crossways slices.

3

Heat the oil in a frying pan over low heat. Put in half the onions and chillies, and cook until soft.

4

Pour in one of the egg mixtures. Cook gently, tilting the pan and lifting the edges of the setting omelette so that as much of the mixture as possible reaches the sides and base of the pan. When done, the top of the omelette should be set and the underside golden brown. Ease the omelette on to a warm plate.

5

Cook the second omelette in the same way.

6

Cut each in half for serving.

Note: Not suitable for freezing.

CHILLI EGGS IN COCONUT MILK

Indonesia

Imperial (Metric)	American
8 hard-boiled eggs	8 hard-boiled eggs
2 teaspoons chilli powder	2 teaspoons chili powder
2 macadamia nuts or blanched almonds	2 macadamia nuts or blanched almonds
1 medium onion, finely chopped	1 medium onion, finely chopped
3 garlic cloves, crushed	3 garlic cloves, crushed
2 tablespoons groundnut oil	2 tablespoons peanut oil
12 fl ounces (340ml) medium-thick coconut milk	1½ cups medium-thick coconut milk
½ teaspoon Laos powder	½ teaspoon Laos powder
1½ stalks lemon grass, finely chopped	1½ stalks lemon grass, finely chopped
3 curry leaves	3 curry leaves

1

Peel the eggs.

2

Put the chilli powder, nuts, onion, garlic and oil in a blender or food processor. Work to a paste.

3

Put the paste in a wok or large frying pan. Set over medium heat and cook, stirring, until it browns.

4

Pour in the coconut milk. Add the Laos powder, lemon grass and curry leaves. Bring the mixture to a boil.

5

Put in the eggs, and cook over medium heat, stirring, until the sauce thickens and reduces by about two thirds.

Note: Not suitable for freezing.

CHILLI OMELETTES

Malaya

These are very similar to the preceding. No soy sauce is used. The sliced chillies and onion, plus 2 chopped spring onions (scallions), are mixed into the beaten eggs, and the mixture is cooked over high heat.

Note: If you are not used to the hot flavour of fresh chillies, it would be a good idea if you halved the amounts when making these omelettes for the first time. If you like them, add more the next time.

SPICED EGGS
WITH COOKED SALAD

Indonesia

Imperial (Metric)	American
8 eggs, hard-boiled	8 hard-boiled eggs
1 tablespoon groundnut oil	1 tablespoon peanut oil
1 small onion, grated	1 small onion, grated
1 garlic clove, grated	1 garlic clove, crushed
½ teaspoon ground ginger	½ teaspoon ground ginger
1 stem lemon grass, bruised	1 stem lemon grass, bruised
3 fl ounces (90ml) tamari or shoyu sauce	⅓ cup tamari or shoyu sauce
4 tablespoons water	4 tablespoons water
Salad:	Salad:
6 ounces (170g) bean sprouts	3 cups bean sprouts
½ Chinese cabbage, shredded	½ Chinese cabbage, shredded
8 ounces (225g) carrots, cut into matchstick pieces	3 medium carrots, cut into matchstick pieces
½ cucumber, thinly sliced	½ cucumber, thinly sliced
4 tablespoons crunchy peanut butter	4 tablespoons crunchy peanut butter
4 fl ounces (125ml) groundnut oil	½ cup peanut oil
Juice of 1 lemon	Juice of 1 lemon
1 garlic clove, crushed	1 garlic clove, crushed
Pinch of chilli powder	Pinch of chili powder
1 small onion, very finely chopped (optional)	1 small onion, very finely chopped (optional)

1

Peel the eggs, and score them all over with a fork.

2

Heat the oil in a wok or frying pan over low heat. Put in the onion and garlic, and cook until very soft.

3

Add the ginger, and cook $\frac{1}{2}$ minute, stirring.

4

Add the lemon grass, soy sauce and water. Bring the mixture to a boil.

5

Put in the eggs. Simmer, turning frequently, for about 20 minutes, or until all the liquid has evaporated. Take the eggs out, and cool completely.

6

Bring three separate pans of lightly salted water to a boil. Put the bean sprouts in one. Cook for 1 minute, drain, run cold water through them, and drain again. Put the Chinese cabbage into another. Cook for $1\frac{1}{2}$ minutes. Drain, run cold water through it, and drain again. Put the carrots in the remaining pan. Cook for 2 minutes. Drain, run cold water through them, and drain again.

7

For the dressing, put the peanut butter in a bowl. Gradually beat in the oil. Stir in the lemon juice, garlic, chilli powder and onion, if using.

8

Quarter the eggs lengthways, and put them in the centre of a very large serving plate. Surround with the bean sprouts, then a ring of carrots, and then the cabbage. Garnish with cucumber rings.

9

Serve the dressing separately.

Note: Not suitable for freezing.

Chapter 3
Bean Curd Dishes

Bean curd is one of the main sources of protein in eastern countries. It is, in fact, a soya bean cheese that looks like a thick, white junket or a block of curds surrounded by whey. It is available fresh from Chinese and Japanese food shops and also from wholefood shops. The Japanese word for bean curd is tofu, and it is under this name that you will most probably find it.

Bean curd has a soft, mild flavour that will lend itself to any herbs, spices or sauces that are added to it. This makes it an extremely versatile ingredient, which can be made into many different types of dishes.

Dried bean curd skin is available in flat sheets or rolls. They are a creamy yellow in colour and must be soaked in warm water about 30 minutes before using.

Fermented bean curd is also called bean curd cheese. It is made by fermenting small cubes of bean curd in wine and salt. It is available in tins and should be used very sparingly with dishes such as Congee (page 126).

STIR-FRIED BEAN CURD WITH MUSHROOMS AND SPRING ONIONS (SCALLIONS)

China

Imperial (Metric)	American
1 pound 4 ounces (565g) bean curd	1¼ pound bean curd
8 ounces (225g) mushrooms	2 cups mushrooms
10 spring onions	10 scallions
2 tablespoons groundnut oil	2 tablespoons peanut oil
2 tablespoons tamari or shoyu sauce	2 tablespoons tamari or shoyu sauce

1

Cut the bean curd into 1-inch (2.5 cm) squares, ¼-inch (6mm) thick.

2

Thinly slice the mushrooms. Cut the scallions into 1-inch (2.5 cm) lengths.

3

Heat the oil in a wok or large frying pan over a high heat. Put in the mushrooms and spring onions (scallions), and stir-fry 1 minute.

4

Add the bean curd, and stir gently 2 minutes, trying not to break it up.

5

Add the soy sauce, and stir 1 minute. Serve immediately.

Note: Not suitable for freezing.

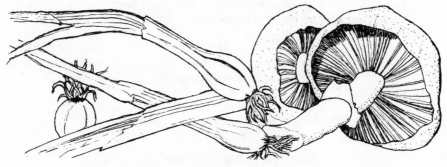

FRIED BEAN CURD WITH HOISIN SAUCE

China

Imperial (Metric)	American
1 pound 4 ounces (565g) bean curd	1¼ pounds bean curd
4 spring onions	4 scallions
½ ounce (15g) fresh ginger root	½ ounce fresh ginger
2 tablespoons Chinese rice wine or dry sherry	2 tablespoons Chinese rice wine or dry sherry
2 tablespoons vegetable stock	2 tablespoons vegetable stock
2 tablespoons hoisin sauce	2 tablespoons hoisin sauce
2 tablespoons tamari or shoyu sauce	2 tablespoons tamari or shoyu sauce
4 tablespoons groundnut oil	4 tablespoons peanut oil
1 garlic clove, crushed	1 garlic clove, crushed

1

Cut the bean curd into ¾-inch (2 cm) cubes. Cut the spring onions (scallions) into 1-inch (2.5 cm) lengths.

2

Peel and grate the ginger root.

3

Mix together the wine or sherry and stock.

4

Mix together the hoisin sauce and tamari or shoyu sauce.

5

Heat the oil in a wok or large frying pan over high heat. Put in the ginger root, spring onions (scallions) and garlic, and stir-fry 15 seconds.

6

Put in the bean curd, and stir-fry 2 minutes. Add the wine or sherry and stock, and stir 1 minute.

7

Stir in the hoisin sauce mixture. Heat through, and remove the pan from the heat.

Note: Not suitable for freezing.

BEAN CURD WITH BLACK BEANS

China

Imperial (Metric)	American
1 pound 4 ounces (565g) bean curd	1¼ pounds bean curd
4 spring onions	4 scallions
3 tablespoons groundnut oil	3 tablespoons peanut oil
2 tablespoons salted black beans	2 tablespoons salted black beans
2 teaspoons chilli sauce	2 teaspoons chilli sauce
2 tablespoons vegetable stock	2 tablespoons vegetable stock
1 tablespoon tamari or shoyu sauce	1 tablespoon tamari or shoyu sauce
Freshly ground Szechuan pepper, if available	Freshly ground Szechuan pepper, if available.

1

Cut the bean curd into ½-inch (1.5 cm) cubes. Bring a pan of water to a boil. Put in the bean curd, cook 2 minutes, and drain.

2

Cut the spring onions (scallions) into ½-inch (1.5 cm) lengths.

3

Heat the oil in a wok or large frying pan over high heat. Put in the beans. Stir-fry 1 minute, and crush them while they are still in the pan. Add the chilli sauce.

4

Put in the stock, bean curd, and spring onions (scallions). Cook over low heat 2 minutes, stirring frequently.

5

Turn the bean curd into a serving dish, and grind the Szechuan pepper over it. If no Szechuan pepper is available, a very little ordinary black pepper may be used.

Note: Not suitable for freezing.

POT-STUCK BEAN CURD WITH LEEKS

China

Imperial (Metric)	American
1 pound 4 ounces (565g) bean curd	1¼ lb bean curd
12 ounces (340g) leeks	2 medium leeks
3 eggs	3 eggs
1 ounce (30g) wholewheat flour	2 tablespoons whole wheat flour
Pinch of fine sea salt	Pinch of fine sea salt
4 tablespoons groundnut oil	4 tablespoons peanut oil
½ pint (285ml) vegetable stock	1⅓ cups vegetable stock
2 tablespoons tamari or shoyu sauce	2 tablespoons tamari or shoyu sauce
2 tablespoons Chinese rice wine or dry sherry	2 tablespoons Chinese rice wine or dry sherry
2 tablespoons arrowroot mixed with 2 tablespoons cold water	2 tablespoons arrowroot mixed with 2 tablespoons cold water

1

Wrap the bean curd in muslin or a clean linen tea cloth. Press it gently to drain off any liquid. Cut into 1-inch (2.5 cm) squares ½-inch (1.5 cm) thick.

2

Thinly slice the leeks. Beat together the eggs, flour and salt.

3

Heat half the oil in a wok or large frying pan over high heat. Dip the pieces of bean curd in the egg mixture. Sauté the pieces until they are golden brown on each side, in several batches if necessary.

4

Clean the pan, and put in the remaining oil. Set over high heat. Put in the leeks, and stir-fry 1 minute.

5

Pour in the stock, and add the tamari or shoyu sauce and wine or sherry. Bring to a boil. Stir in the arrowroot mixture, and stir until the sauce thickens. Put the bean curd into the sauce. Simmer 1 minute. Serve as soon as possible.

Note: Not suitable for freezing.

DEEP-FRIED BEAN CURD WITH CHILLI AND YELLOW BEAN SAUCE

China

Imperial (Metric)	American
1 pound 4 ounces (565g) bean curd	1¼ pounds bean curd
2 red chillies	2 red chilis
6 spring onions	6 scallions
Oil for deep-frying	Oil for deep-frying
1 tablespoon groundnut oil	1 tablespoon peanut oil
1 tablespoon Chinese rice wine or dry sherry	1 tablespoon Chinese rice wine or dry sherry
1 tablespoon tamari or shoyu sauce	1 tablespoon tamari or shoyu sauce
2 tablespoons yellow bean sauce	2 tablespoons yellow bean sauce
¼ teaspoon sesame oil	¼ teaspoon sesame oil

1

Cut the bean curd into slices about 1 inch by 2 inches (2.5 by 5 cm) and ¼-inch (6 mm) thick.

2

Core, seed and finely chop the chillies. Cut the spring onions (scallions) into 1-inch (2.5 cm) lengths.

3

Heat the oil for deep-frying to 350F/180C. Drop in the pieces of bean curd about six at a time and deep-fry until golden brown. Remove, and drain on paper towels.

4

Heat the 1 tablespoon oil in a wok or large frying pan over high heat. Put in the chillies and spring onions (scallions), and stir-fry 1 minute.

5

Add the wine or sherry, tamari or shoyu sauce and yellow bean sauce. Put in the bean curd, and simmer 3 minutes.

6

Sprinkle in the sesame oil. Serve as soon as possible.

Note: Not suitable for freezing.

DEEP-FRIED BEAN CURD WITH MUSHROOMS, BAMBOO SHOOTS AND BEAN SPROUTS

China

Imperial (Metric)	American
4 Chinese mushrooms	4 Chinese mushrooms
1 pound 4 ounces (565g) bean curd	1¼ pounds bean curd
2 teaspoons fine sea salt	2 teaspoons fine sea salt
4 ounces (115g) drained, tinned bamboo shoots	1 cup drained, canned bamboo shoots
4 spring onions	4 scallions
Oil for deep frying	Oil for deep frying
2 tablespoons groundnut oil	2 tablespoons peanut oil
1 garlic clove, crushed	1 garlic clove, crushed
4 ounces (115g) bean sprouts	2 cups bean sprouts
3 tablespoons tamari or shoyu sauce	3 tablespoons tamari or shoyu sauce
1 tablespoon Chinese rice wine or dry sherry	1 tablespoon Chinese rice wine or dry sherry
8 fl ounces (225ml) vegetable stock	1 cup vegetable stock

1

Soak the mushrooms in hot water 30 minutes. Drain, and quarter.

2

Cut the bean curd into four flat cakes. Lay them on a plate. Sprinkle with the salt, and let sit 1 minute. Drain the water from the plate.

3

Thinly slice the bamboo shoots. Chop the onions into 1-inch (2.5cm) lengths.

4

Heat the oil for deep-frying to a temperature of 350F/180C. Put in the pieces of bean curd one at a time, and fry until golden. Lift out on to paper towels.

5

Heat the 2 tablespoons oil in a wok or large frying pan over high heat. Put in the garlic, and cook 30 seconds. Put in the mushrooms, spring onions (scallions), bamboo shoots and bean sprouts. Stir-fry 30 seconds.

6

Put in the bean curd, tamari or shoyu sauce, sherry and stock.

7

Cover and simmer 10 to 15 minutes, or until the sauce is thick.

Note: Not suitable for freezing.

CLEAR-SIMMERED BEAN CURD WITH CHINESE CABBAGE AND CUCUMBER

China

Imperial (Metric)	American
2 ounces (55g) transparent noodles	2 ounces transparent noodles
1 pound 4 ounces (565g) bean curd	1¼ pound bean curd
8 ounces (225g) Chinese cabbage	½ pound Chinese Cabbage
½ medium-sized cucumber	¼ medium-sized cucumber
1¼ pints (850ml) vegetable stock	3¾ cups vegetable stock
2 tablespoons tamari or shoyu sauce	2 tablespoons tamari or shoyu sauce
2 tablespoons Chinese rice wine or dry sherry	2 tablespoons Chinese rice wine or dry sherry
1 teaspoon sesame oil	1 teaspoon sesame oil

1

Soak the noodles in warm water for 10 minutes. Drain.

2

Cut the bean curd into pieces about 2 inches by 1 inch (5 cm by 2.5 cm) and 1-inch (2.5 cm) thick.

3

Cut each Chinese cabbage leaf in half slantways across the stem.

4

Cut the cucumber into pieces 2 by 1 by ½ inch (5 by 2.5 by 1.5 cm).

5

Put the bean curd in a heatproof bowl or dish with the noodles, cabbage and cucumber. Pour in the stock, and add the tamari or shoyu sauce, wine or sherry and sesame oil. Cover the bowl with foil, and put in a large steamer.

6

Bring a pan of water to a boil. Lower in the steamer. Cover and cook 30 minutes.

Take the bowl to the table. Ladle the bean curd, broth and vegetables into bowls.

Note: Not suitable for freezing.

STEAMED BEAN CURD WITH COCONUT AND CHILLI

Indonesia

Imperial (Metric)	American
1 pound (455g) bean curd	1 pound bean curd
4 spring onions, finely chopped	4 scallions, finely chopped
2 garlic cloves, crushed	2 garlic cloves, crushed
1 teaspoon ground coriander	1 teaspoon ground coriander
1 tablespoon lime juice	1 tablespoon lime juice
8 fl ounces (225ml) thick coconut milk	1 cup thick coconut milk
4 green chillies, seeded and finely chopped	4 green chilis, seeded and finely chopped
2 eggs, beaten	2 eggs, beaten
1 tablespoon tamari or shoyu sauce	1 tablespoon tamari or shoyu sauce
Pinch of sea salt	Pinch of sea salt
1 bay leaf	1 bay leaf

1

Put the bean curd into a bowl, and mash it with a fork.

2

Mix in all the other ingredients apart from the bay leaf.

3

Pour the mixture into a soufflée dish, and put the bay leaf on top. Put the dish in a steamer.

4

Bring a large pan of water to a boil. Lower in the steamer. Cover and cook for 45 minutes or until the mixture has set.

Note: Not suitable for freezing.

DEEP-FRIED BEAN CURD WITH SOY SAUCE

Japan

Imperial (Metric)	American
1 pound 4 ounces (565g) bean curd	1¼ pounds bean curd
Sauce:	Sauce:
3 tablespoons sake or dry sherry	3 tablespoons sake or dry sherry
3 fl ounces (90ml) tamari or shoyu sauce	⅓ cup tamari or shoyu sauce
4 fl ounces (125ml) kombu stock	½ cup kombu stock
5 teaspoons flaked, dried bonito	5 teaspoons flaked, dried bonito
Garnish:	Garnish:
4 ounces (115g) mooli (Japanese white radish)	¼ pound mooli (Japanese white radish)
1 ounce (30g) fresh ginger root	1 ounce fresh ginger

1

Make the sauce. Heat the sake or sherry in a saucepan over moderate heat until lukewarm. Ignite it, and shake the pan gently until the flame dies. Add half the tamari or shoyu sauce, the kombu stock and dried bonito. Bring to a boil, and then strain through a sieve. Cool completely, and add the remaining tamari or shoyu sauce.

2

For the garnish, finely grate the mooli and ginger root separately.

3

Cut the bean curd into slices 2 by 1 inch (5 × 2.5 cm) and ¼-inch (6 mm) thick. Dry with towels.

4

Heat a pan of hot oil to 350F/180C. Fry the bean curd pieces, about 6 at a time, until golden. Drain on paper towels.

5

Arrange the fried bean curd on four dinner plates, putting a small pile of mooli and one of grated ginger beside each portion. Serve the sauce separately, if possible, in four tiny bowls.

Note: Not suitable for freezing.

BEAN CURD OMELETTE

Indonesia

Serves 2

Imperial (Metric)	American
8 ounces (225g) bean curd	½ pound bean curd
2 eggs	2 eggs
2 tablespoons groundnut oil	2 tablespoons peanut oil
2 tablespoons tamari or shoyu sauce	2 tablespoons tamari or shoyu sauce
2 teaspoons crunchy peanut butter	2 teaspoons crunchy peanut butter

1

Cut the bean curd into ½-inch (1.5 cm) dice. Put it into a sieve, and leave it over a bowl for 10 minutes so any excess water can drain from it.

2

Lightly beat the eggs. Mix in the bean curd.

3

Preheat the grill (broiler) to high. Heat the oil in a frying pan over medium heat. Pour in the egg and bean curd mixture. Cook, tipping the pan and lifting the sides of the setting egg, until the underside is set and beginning to colour.

4

Transfer the pan to the grill (broiler). Cook until the omelette is set and the top browned.

5

Work the tamari or shoyu sauce and peanut butter together in a blender. Spoon the mixture over the omelette before serving.

Note: Not suitable for freezing.

THE MONK'S SIMMERED VEGETABLES

China

Imperial (Metric)	American
12 ounces (340g) bean curd	¾ pound bean curd
6 Chinese mushrooms	6 Chinese mushrooms
3 ounces (85g) transparent noodles	¼ pound transparent noodles
8 ounces (225g) small carrots	2 to 3 small carrots
8 ounces (225g) small courgettes	2 small zucchini
8 ounces (225g) French beans	1½ cups French beans
8 ounces (225g) Chinese cabbage	½ pound Chinese cabbage
Oil for deep-frying	Oil for deep-frying
1 pint (570ml) vegetable stock	2½ cups vegetable stock
2 tablespoons tamari or shoyu sauce	2 tablespoons tamari or shoyu sauce
2 tablespoons Chinese rice wine or dry sherry	2 tablespoons Chinese rice wine or dry sherry
2 tablespoons hoisin sauce	2 tablespoons hoisin sauce
1 tablespoon sesame oil	1 tablespoon sesame oil
4 spring onions, chopped	4 scallions, chopped

1

Cut the bean curd into 1-inch (2.5 cm) cubes.

2

Soak the mushrooms in ¼ pint (140 ml or ½ cup) hot water for 30 minutes. Drain, reserving the water. Quarter the mushrooms.

3

Soak the noodles in warm water for 5 minutes. Drain.

4

Cut the carrots into pieces. Make the first cut at a 45° angle to the side of the carrot and slanting upwards; the next at the same angle but slanting downwards so you get small triangular pieces.

5

Cut the courgettes (zucchini) in the same way.

6

Top and tail the beans, and cut them into 1-inch (2.5 cm) lengths.

7

Cut the cabbage into 1-inch (2.5 cm) squares.

8

Deep-fry the pieces of bean curd until golden brown. Drain on paper towels.

9

Bring the stock to a boil in a large pan. Add the mushroom water, tamari or shoyu sauce, rice wine or sherry and hoisin sauce. Put in the mushrooms and carrots, cover and cook 5 minutes. Add the courgettes (zucchini) and French beans, and cook a further 5 minutes. Add the cabbage, and cook 5 minutes more. Finally, put in the noodles and bean curd, and cook a final 5 minutes.

10

Transfer the vegetables to a large tureen. Scatter the sesame oil and spring onions (scallions) over the top.

Note: Not suitable for freezing.

BEAN CURD AND COOKED VEGETABLE SALAD

Indonesia

Imperial (Metric)	American
12 ounces (340g) bean curd	¾ pound bean curd
12 ounces (340g) waxy potatoes	5 to 6 new potatoes
8 ounces (225g) French beans	½ cup French beans
8 ounces (225g) Chinese cabbage	½ pound Chinese cabbage
8 ounces (225g) carrots	2 to 3 small carrots
½ cucumber	½ cucumber
Oil for deep-frying	Oil for deep-frying
Sauce:	Sauce:
2 tablespoons groundnut oil	2 tablespoons peanut oil
4 red chillies	4 red chilis
2 garlic cloves, crushed	2 garlic cloves, crushed
4 ounces (115g) peanut butter	1 cup peanut butter
8 fl ounces (225ml) thick coconut milk	1 cup thick coconut milk
2 tablespoons tamari or shoyu sauce	2 tablespoons tamari or shoyu sauce
½ teaspoon Laos powder	½ teaspoon Laos powder
2 curry leaves	2 curry leaves
1 teaspoon lemon juice	1 teaspoon lemon juice

1

Make the sauce. Heat the oil in a wok or frying pan over low heat. Put in the chillies and garlic. Fry for 2 minutes. Put them into a blender and grind finely. Add the peanut butter, coconut milk and tamari or shoyu sauce. Blend well. Put the mixture in a saucepan. Add the Laos powder and curry leaves, and bring to a boil. Cook gently until the sauce thickens slightly. It should be of a pouring consistency. If too thick, add a little water. Take the pan from the heat, and stir in the lemon juice.

2

Cut the bean curd into ½-inch (1.5 cm) dice.

3

Boil the potatoes in their skins until just tender. Peel and dice them as soon as they are cool enough to handle.

4

Top and tail the beans. Break into 1-inch (2.5 cm) lengths. Blanch in boiling water for 3 minutes. Drain, run cold water through them, and drain again.

5

Finely shred the cabbage. Blanch in boiling water for 1 minute. Drain it, run cold water through it, and drain again.

6

Cut the carrots into thin, diagonal slices. Blanch in boiling water 3 minutes. Drain, run cold water through them, and drain again.

7

Cut the cucumber into 1-inch by $\frac{1}{2}$-inch (2.5 cm by 1.5 cm) pieces.

8

Heat a pan of deep oil to 350F/180C. Put in the bean curd, diced and cook until golden. Drain paper towels, and put them in the centre of a very large serving plate.

9

Arrange the other vegetables in rings around them. French beans, potatoes, cabbage, carrots, cucumber.

10

Traditionally, the sauce is poured over the vegetables before serving. However, as it has a distinctive, hot flavour, it would be best to serve it separately.

Note: Not suitable for freezing.

BEAN CURD AND PEANUT SALAD

China

Imperial (Metric)	American
1 pound (455g) bean curd	1 pound bean curd
½ medium cucumber	½ medium cucumber
4 ounces (115g) peanuts	¾ cup peanuts
Oil for deep-frying	Oil for deep-frying
Dressing:	Dressing:
2 tablespoons tahini (sesame paste)	2 tablespoons tahini (sesame paste)
1 tablespoon tamari or shoyu sauce	1 tablespoon tamari or shoyu sauce
1 tablespoon white wine vinegar	1 tablespoon white wine vinegar
1 tablespoon rice wine or dry sherry	1 tablespoon rice wine or dry sherry
1 teaspoon chilli sauce	1 teaspoon chili sauce
1 garlic clove, crushed with a pinch of fine sea salt	1 garlic clove, crushed with a pinch of fine sea salt
2 tablespoons cold water	2 tablespoons cold water

1

Make the dressing. Put the tahini in a bowl, and gradually work in the remaining ingredients to give the consistency of thick mayonnaise.

2

Cut the bean curd and the cucumber into ½-inch (1.5 cm) dice. Put the cucumber and peanuts into a bowl.

3

Heat a pan of deep oil to 350F/180C. Put in the cubes of bean curd, and fry them until they are just turning brown. Remove, and drain on paper towels.

4

Quickly mix the bean curd into the cucumber and peanuts. Mix in the dressing. Serve immediately; if the bean curd is left too long, it will lose its crispness.

Note: Not suitable for freezing.

BEAN CURD AND SPINACH SALAD

China

Imperial (Metric)	American
1 pound 4 ounces (565g) bean curd	1¼ pounds bean curd
1 pound (455g) spinach	4 cups spinach
2 tablespoons tamari or shoyu sauce	2 tablespoons tamari or shoyu sauce
1 tablespoon sesame oil	1 tablespoon sesame oil
1 tablespoon white wine vinegar	1 tablespoon white wine vinegar

1

Put the bean curd in a bowl. Pour boiling water over it. Leave for 30 seconds. Drain, and cut into shreds.

2

Bring a large saucepan of water to a boil. Put in the spinach, and bring it back to a boil. Take the pan from the heat. Drain and cool the spinach. Squeeze out any excess water.

3

In a bowl, mix the spinach with the bean curd.

4

Mix together the sauce, sesame oil and vinegar. Fold the mixture into the spinach and bean curd. Serve cool.

Note: Not suitable for freezing.

BUDDHA'S FRY

China

Imperial (Metric)	American
2 ounces (55g) dried bean curd skin	2 ounces dried bean curd skin
6 dried Chinese mushrooms	6 dried Chinese mushrooms
1 ounce (30g) transparent noodles	1 ounce transparent noodles
2 ounces (55g) Chinese cabbage	2 ounces Chinese cabbage
2 ounces (55g) carrots	½ small carrot
2 ounces (55g) bamboo shoots	¼ cup bamboo shoots
4 ounces (115g) mangetout peas	¼ cup snow peas
2 ounces (55g) broccoli or cauliflower	½ cup broccoli or cauliflower
6 water chestnuts	6 water chestnuts
1 ounce (30g) tinned lily root	1 ounce canned lily root
4 tablespoons groundnut oil	4 tablespoons peanut oil
2 ounces (55g) bean sprouts	1 cup bean sprouts
2 tablespoons tamari or shoyu sauce	2 tablespoons tamari or shoyu sauce
1 tablespoon arrowroot, mixed with 2 tablespoons water	1 tablespoon arrowroot mixed with 2 tablespoons water
1 tablespoon sesame oil	1 tablespoon sesame oil

1

Soak the bean curd skin in hot water for 30 minutes. Drain, and cut into 1-inch (2.5 cm) squares.

2

Soak the mushrooms in ½ pint (285 ml or 1⅓ cups) hot water for 30 minutes. Drain, reserving the water. Quarter.

3

Soak the noodles in hot water for 5 minutes. Drain, and cut into 1-inch (2.5 cm) lengths.

4

Cut the Chinese cabbage into 1-inch (2.5 cm) squares.

5

Cut the carrots into thin, diagonal slices.

6

Thinly slice the bamboo shoots.

7

Top and tail the mangetout (snow) peas.

8

Cut the cauliflower or broccoli into small florettes.

9

Thinly slice the water chestnuts and lily root.

10

Heat the oil in a wok or large frying pan over high heat. Put in the mushrooms, cabbage, carrots, mangetout (snow) peas and broccoli, and stir-fry 2 minutes.

11

Put in the bean curd, transparent noodles, bamboo shoots, water chestnuts, lily root and bean sprouts. Stir-fry a further 2 minutes.

12

Pour in the mushroom water and tamari or shoyu sauce. Bring to a boil. Stir in the arrowroot mixture, and stir until the sauce thickens.

13

Cover, and simmer for 10 minutes.

14

Add the sesame oil, and mix well.

15

Serve with rice.

Note: Not suitable for freezing.

Chapter 4
Nuts

Although nuts grow in eastern countries, they are seldom used alone in dishes such as a western nut roast. The stir-fried almonds and stir-fried and stir-braised cashew nuts in this chapter are my own recipes, using various combinations of Chinese ingredients and methods. They taste authentic, but they may not be served on eastern tables. Chestnuts are made into a Chinese dish with pork and Chinese cabbage. I have simply omitted the pork and have used more chestnuts, again producing a dish with a genuine Chinese flavour.

Peanuts are frequently used in Southeast Asian cooking for grinding and mixing with spices and other ingredients to make rich sauces for plainly cooked vegetables. Besides the recipes in this chapter, see Spiced Eggs with Cooked Salad (page 52) and Bean Curd and Cooked Vegetable Salad (page 68).

Coconut is also frequently used in sauces. It can also make really substantial family meals such as the Vegetable, Coconut and Egg Bake.

The savoury roasted peanuts from China are best served with drinks or Chinese tea before a meal.

PEANUTS ROASTED WITH RED BEAN-CURD CHEESE

China

Imperial (Metric)	American
8 ounces (225g) peanuts	1½ cups peanuts
2 tablespoons mashed red bean-curd cheese	2 tablespoons mashed red bean curd cheese
1 teaspoon Barbados sugar	1 teaspoon brown sugar
4 tablespoons water	4 tablespoons water

1

Heat the oven to 300F/150C gas 2.

2

Put the peanuts, bean-curd cheese, sugar and water into a saucepan. Bring to a boil, and cook for 2 minutes, stirring so all the liquid evaporates.

3

Spread the coated nuts on a baking sheet. Put them in the oven for 20 minutes, turning several times. They should be quite dry.

4

Turn the peanuts on to a tray or plate and let cool. Store in an airtight jar.

LONGEVITY NUTS

China

Imperial (Metric)	American
8 ounces (225g) peanuts	1½ cups peanuts
3 fl ounces (90ml) groundnut oil	⅓ cup peanut oil
2 teaspoons Barbados sugar	2 teaspoons brown sugar
¼ teaspoon five-spice powder	¼ teaspoon five-spice powder
½ teaspoon Szechuan pepper and salt mixture	½ teaspoon Szechuan pepper and salt mixture

1

Cover a large tray with a double layer of paper towels.

2

Heat half the oil in a wok or large frying pan over high heat. Put in half the nuts, and stir-fry 1 minute or until they begin to brown. Using a slotted spoon, lift them out on to the paper towels.

3

Cook the remaining nuts in the same way, and drain them on the paper.

4

Tip all the nuts into a bowl. Mix in the sugar, five-spice powder and Szechuan pepper and salt mixture.

5

Cool the nuts completely.

6

Store in airtight jars.

STIR-FRIED CASHEW NUTS WITH SPINACH

China

Imperial (Metric)	American
1 pound (455g) spinach	4 cups spinach
4 spring onions	4 scallions
4 tablespoons groundnut oil	4 tablespoons peanut oil
4 ounces (115g) cashew nuts or cashew nut pieces	¾ cup cashew nuts or cashew nut pieces
1 garlic clove, finely chopped	1 garlic clove, finely chopped
2 tablespoons tamari or shoyu sauce	2 tablespoons tamari or shoyu sauce
2 tablespoons Chinese rice wine or dry sherry	2 tablespoons Chinese rice wine or dry sherry

1

Cut the stalks off the spinach where they meet the leaves. Chop the leaves. Cut the spring onions (scallions) into 1-inch (2.5 cm) lengths.

2

Heat the oil in a wok or large frying pan over high heat. Put in the cashew nuts, and stir-fry until they begin to brown, about 1½ minutes. Remove.

3

Put the garlic into the pan, and stir-fry 30 seconds. Put in the spinach and spring onions (scallions). Stir-fry about 3 minutes, or until the spinach just begins to soften.

4

Mix in the cashew nuts.

5

Pour in the tamari or shoyu sauce and rice wine or sherry. Stir-fry 1 minute more. Take the pan from the heat, and serve as soon as possible.

Note: Not suitable for freezing.

STIR-FRIED ALMONDS WITH ASPARAGUS AND FRENCH BEANS

China

Imperial (Metric)	American
4 ounces (115g) almonds	1 cup almonds
1 pound (455g) asparagus	1 pound asparagus
8 ounces (225g) French beans	1½ cups French beans
4 spring onions	4 scallions
4 tablespoons groundnut oil	4 tablespoons peanut oil
2 tablespoons tamari or shoyu sauce	2 tablespoons tamari or shoyu sauce
2 tablespoons Chinese rice wine or dry sherry	2 tablespoons Chinese rice wine or dry sherry

1

Put the almonds in a shallow pan, and cover with cold water. Bring to a boil over high heat. Drain and squeeze from their skins.

2

Use only the top 4 inches (10 cm) of the asparagus. Cut these tips off diagonally, and then cut each one diagonally in half.

3

Top and tail the beans. Cut into 2-inch (5 cm) lengths.

4

Cut the spring onions (scallions) diagonally into 2-inch (5 cm) lengths.

5

Bring two separate pans of water to a boil. Put the beans in one and the asparagus in the other. Cook them each for 2 minutes. Drain.

6

Heat half the oil in a wok or large frying pan over medium heat. Put in the almonds, and stir-fry about 2 minutes, or until golden brown. Remove.

7

Put the remaining oil in the pan. Put in the asparagus and beans, and stir-fry 4 to 5 minutes so the asparagus becomes bright green.

8

Pour in the tamari or shoyu sauce and rice wine or sherry. Stir-fry 1 minute more.

9

Put the vegetables into a serving dish, and scatter the browned almonds over the top.

Note: Not suitable for freezing.

TEA-SIMMERED CHESTNUTS

Japan

Imperial (Metric)	American
12 chestnuts	12 chestnuts
1 tablespoon Japanese green tea leaves	1 tablespoon Japanese green tea leaves
1 tablespoon Barbados sugar	1 tablespoon brown sugar
1 teaspoon tamari or shoyu sauce	1 teaspoon tamari or shoyu sauce

1

Slit the tops of the chestnuts. Put the chestnuts in a saucepan, and cover with cold water. Bring to a boil, and cook briskly for 2 minutes. Drain and peel them, leaving the brown membrane intact.

2

Put the peeled chestnuts in a saucepan with the tea leaves. Cover with cold water. Bring to a boil, cover, and simmer 20 minutes, or until they can be pierced with a sharp knife but still hold their shape. Drain.

3

Put the chestnuts back in the saucepan with 8 fl ounces (225ml or 1 cup) water and the sugar. Bring to a boil and simmer uncovered, 20 minutes.

4

Stir in the tamari or shoyu sauce. Simmer a further 5 minutes. Take the pan from the heat. Cool the chestnuts to room temperature in the liquid. Drain just before serving.

Note: Not suitable for freezing.

STIR-FRIED SWEET AND SOUR ALMONDS

China

Imperial (Metric)	American
4 ounces (115g) almonds	1 cup almonds
½ small pineapple	½ small pineapple
1 green pepper	1 sweet green pepper
1 large onion	1 large onion
One 8 ounce (225g) tin bamboo shoots	2 cups bamboo shoots
One 8 ounce (225g) tin water chestnuts	2 cups canned water chestnuts
1 tablespoon arrowroot	1 tablespoon arrowroot
2 teaspoons tamari or shoyu sauce	2 teaspoons tamari or shoyu sauce
5 tablespoons cider vinegar	5 tablespoons cider vinegar
1 tablespoon clear honey	1 tablespoon clear honey
3 tablespoons groundnut oil	3 tablespoons peanut oil
1 garlic clove, finely chopped	1 garlic clove, finely chopped

1

Put the almonds in a shallow pan, and cover with cold water. Bring to a boil. Drain, squeeze them from their skins.

2

Cut the husk from the pineapple. Cut the flesh into slices, and stamp out the cores. Cut the pineapple into ¾-inch (2 cm) dice.

3

Core and seed the pepper, and cut it into ¾-inch (2 cm) squares.

4

Thinly slice the onion.

5

Drain the bamboo shoots and water chestnuts, and thinly slice.

6

Put the arrowroot in a bowl. Gradually mix in the tamari or shoyu sauce, vinegar and honey.

7

Heat the oil in a wok or large frying pan over low heat. Put in the pepper, onion and garlic and stir-fry 2 minutes. Put in the almonds, bamboo shoots and water chestnuts and stir-fry 2 minutes more.

8

Mix in the pineapple.

9

Give the arrowroot mixture a stir. Pour it into the pan. Simmer, stirring until the mixture thickens to make a small amount of glossy sauce. Take the pan from the heat, and serve as soon as possible.

Note: Not suitable for freezing.

CASHEW NUTS STIR-BRAISED WITH MIXED VEGETABLES

China

Imperial (Metric)	American
½ medium-sized cauliflower	½ medium-sized cauliflower
4 ounces (115g) carrots	1 to 2 small carrots
4 celery sticks	4 celery stalks
1 large onion	1 large onion
1 tablespoon arrowroot	1 tablespoon arrowroot
4 tablespoons Chinese rice wine or dry sherry	4 tablespoons Chinese rice wine or dry sherry
½ pint (285ml) vegetable stock	1⅓ cups vegetable stock
1 tablespoon tamari or shoyu sauce	1 tablespoon tamari or shoyu sauce
3 tablespoons groundnut oil	3 tablespoons peanut oil
1 garlic clove, finely chopped	1 garlic clove, finely chopped
4 ounces (115g) cashew nuts or cashew nut pieces	¾ cup cashew nuts or cashew nut pieces
½ ounce (15g) fresh ginger root, peeled and grated	½ ounce fresh ginger, peeled and grated

1

Cut the cauliflower into small florettes. Cut the carrots into very thin diagonal slices. Cut the celery sticks into ¾-inch (2 cm) squares. Thinly slice the onion.

2

Put the arrowroot in a bowl. Gradually mix in the wine or sherry, stock and tamari or shoyu sauce.

3

Heat the oil in a wok or large frying pan over high heat. Put in the cauliflower, carrots, celery, onion and garlic, and stir-fry 2 minutes. Put in the cashew nuts, and stir-fry 1 minute more. Add the ginger.

4

Lower the heat to medium. Stir the arrowroot mixture, and pour it into the pan. Stir until it comes to a boil. Cover the pan and cook, still over moderate heat, 10 minutes.

Note: Not suitable for freezing.

BRAISED CHESTNUTS WITH CHINESE CABBAGE

China

Imperial (Metric)	American
12 ounces (340g) chestnuts	¾ pound chestnuts
12 Chinese mushrooms	12 Chinese mushrooms
1 Chinese cabbage	1 Chinese cabbage
4 tablespoons groundnut oil	4 tablespoons peanut oil
1 garlic clove, finely chopped	1 garlic clove, finely chopped
2 tablespoons tamari or shoyu sauce	2 tablespoons tamari or shoyu sauce

1

Slit the tops of the chestnuts. Put them in a saucepan, and cover with cold water. Bring to a boil, and boil 10 minutes. Peel and cut in half.

2

Soak the mushrooms in warm water for 15 minutes. Drain, reserving the water. Cut each in half.

3

Shred the cabbage.

4

Heat the oil in a wok or large frying pan over high heat. Put in the cabbage and mushrooms and stir-fry 2 minutes. Add 3 tablespoons of the mushroom water and the tamari or shoyu sauce. Cover, and cook over low heat 5 minutes.

5

Put in the chestnuts, cover again, and cook a further 5 minutes.

Note: Not suitable for freezing.

VEGETABLE, COCONUT AND EGG BAKE

Indonesia

Imperial (Metric)	American
Two 8 ounce (225g) tins bamboo shoots	4 cups bamboo shoots
1 medium onion	1 medium onion
2 tablespoons groundnut oil	2 tablespoons peanut oil
2 garlic cloves, crushed	2 garlic cloves, crushed
½ fresh coconut, grated, or 6 oz (170g) desiccated coconut	½ fresh coconut, grated, or 2 cups dried coconut
¼ teaspoon chilli powder	¼ teaspoon chili powder
1 teaspoon paprika	1 teaspoon paprika
½ teaspoon ground ginger	½ teaspoon ground ginger
½ teaspoon ground coriander	½ teaspoon ground coriander
2 teaspoons tomato ketchup	2 teaspoons ketchup
Pinch of sea salt	Pinch of sea salt
8 fl ounces (225ml) water	1 cup water
2 eggs, beaten	2 eggs, beaten

1
Heat the oven to 350F/180C.

2
Thinly slice the bamboo shoots and onion.

3
Heat the oil in a wok or large frying pan. Put in the bamboo shoots, onion and garlic, and stir-fry 1 minute.

4
Mix in the coconut, chilli powder, paprika, ginger, coriander and tomato ketchup. Stir-fry 2 minutes.

5
Pour in the water. Cover, and simmer 5 minutes. Uncover, and stir over heat until all the water has been absorbed. Add salt to taste.

Note: Not suitable for freezing.

7

Transfer the mixture to a 2-inch (5 cm) deep ovenproof dish. Pour the beaten egg over the top.

8

Put the dish into the oven for 30 minutes, or until the egg has set.

BUMBU

Indonesia

Imperial (Metric)	American
½ small fresh coconut	½ small fresh coconut
1 tablespoon tomato ketchup	1 tablespoon ketchup
¼ teaspoon chilli powder	¼ teaspoon chili powder
1 garlic clove	1 garlic clove
Pinch of sea salt	Pinch of sea salt
Juice of ½ lime	Juice of ¼ lime

1

Remove the brown skin from the coconut. Grate the white flesh, and put it in a bowl.

2

Add the tomato ketchup.

3

Pound together the chilli powder, garlic and salt. Add to the coconut.

4

Add the lime juice, and mix well.

Note: Not suitable for freezing.

VEGETABLE SALAD WITH COCONUT DRESSING

Indonesia

The vegetable ingredients for this salad can either be raw or partially cooked so that they are still crisp and fresh.

The cooked vegetables can include:
Shredded green cabbage or Chinese cabbage, shredded and blanched for 1 minute.

French beans or runner beans, cut into 1-inch (2.5 cm) lengths and blanched for 2 minutes.

Carrots, cut diagonally into slices and blanched for 1 minute or into matchstick pieces and blanched for 2 minutes.

Bean sprouts, blanched for 1 minute.

Cauliflower, cut into small florettes and blanched for 2 minutes.

Potatoes, boiled until they are just tender, peeled and sliced or diced.

The raw vegetables can include:
Carrots, chopped, cut into very thin matchstick pieces, or grated.

White cabbage, shredded

Chinese cabbage, shredded

Radishes, sliced

Cucumber, sliced or cut into matchstick pieces.

Spring onions (scallions), chopped or cut into 1-inch (2.5 cm) lengths

Watercress, chopped

Mint, parsley and/or fresh coriander, finely chopped

Choose from both sections of vegetables if wished, or have all raw or all cooked. Mix them together in a large bowl.

The coconut dressing is known as a Bumbu. It should be mixed into the vegetables in the bowl. More fresh parsley, mint or coriander can be scattered over the top.

Note: Not suitable for freezing.

PEANUT AND COCONUT TOPPING FOR RICE

Indonesia

Serve this scattered over yellow rice or rice cooked in coconut milk.

Imperial (Metric)	American
6 ounces (170g) peanuts	1¼ cups peanuts
4 ounces (115g) desiccated coconut	1⅓ cups dried coconut
1 teaspoon ground cumin	1 teaspoon ground cumin
½ teaspoon ground coriander	½ teaspoon ground coriander
1 medium onion, finely chopped	1 medium onion, finely chopped
1 garlic clove, crushed	1 garlic clove, crushed
Juice of ¼ lemon	Juice of ¼ lemon
Oil for greasing	Oil for greasing

1

Put the peanuts in a heavy saucepan, and set over medium heat. Stir until they brown and smell very nutty, about 2 minutes. Tip into a bowl.

2

Mix together all the remaining ingredients apart from the oil.

3

Very lightly grease the frying pan with oil. Set it over very low heat. Put in the coconut mixture. Stir it over low heat about 5 minutes or until it is golden brown.

4

Tip the mixture into the bowl with the peanuts. Cool.

Note: Not suitable for freezing.

MIXED SALAD WITH PEANUT DRESSING

Malaysia

Imperial (Metric)	American
8 ounces (225g) peanuts	1½ cups peanuts
2 ounces (55g) dried tamarind	2 ounces dried tamarind
½ tablespoon chilli powder	½ tablespoon chili powder
½ teaspoon sea salt	½ teaspoon sea salt
1 tablespoon tomato ketchup	1 tablespoon ketchup
8 ounces (225g) green cabbage	3 cups green cabbage, shredded
4 ounces (115g) French beans	¾ cup French beans
8 ounces (225g) potatoes	2 medium potatoes
8 ounces (225g) tinned lotus root	½-pound can lotus root
10 ounces (285g) bean curd	¾ pound bean curd
4 eggs, hard-boiled	4 hard-boiled eggs

1

Heat the oven to 350F/180C gas 4. Spread the nuts on a baking sheet. Put them in the oven for 10 minutes. Tip on to a plate to cool. Grind roughly in a liquidizer (blender) or food processor. Put in a bowl.

2

Put the tamarind in a bowl, and pour on ¼ pint (140ml or ⅔ cup) boiling water. Let sit 10 minutes, and rub it through a sieve.

3

Mix the tamarind water, chilli powder, salt, and ketchup into the peanuts. Add water if necessary to make a sauce of thick pouring consistency.

4

Cook the potatoes in their skins in lightly boiling, salted water for 20 minutes, or until just tender. Drain. Skin them as soon as they are cool enough to handle and dice.

5

Shred the cabbage. Cut the beans into 1-inch (2.5 cm) lengths. Bring two pans of water to a boil. Put the cabbage into one. Cook 1 minute. Drain it, and run cold water through it. Put the beans into another. Cook for 2 minutes, drain, and run cold water through them.

6

Thinly slice the lotus root. Dice the bean curd. Cut the eggs into halves.

7

Arrange the vegetables, eggs and bean curd on a very large platter.

8

Either spoon the sauce over the top or serve it separately.

Note: Not suitable for freezing.

Chapter 5
Vegetable Dishes

There is an absolute wealth of vegetables in eastern countries, and they are nearly always cooked to preserve as much flavour and goodness as possible.

In China and Japan particularly, they are meticulously cut to make them look attractive and also to ensure that they will be suitable for the quick-cooking methods.

In China vegetables are most frequently stir-fried. They can also be stir-braised, which means that after a quick stir-frying process, they are cooked rapidly in just enough liquid to prevent them from sticking. They can also be marinated in a spicy sauce and then deep-fried.

Salads as we know them rarely feature in eastern cuisine. Few vegetables are served completely raw. Instead they are blanched for no more than two minutes in boiling water, drained, cooled and attractively arranged on plates, to be coated with a spicy dressing.

The most famous Japanese recipe of all must be tempura. Surprisingly enough it only arrived in Japan in the seventeenth century, being taken there by the Portuguese, but the Japanese have brought it to utter perfection. Their technique of dropping ice-cold batter into very hot oil makes the final result crisp and light as air.

STIR-FRIED FRENCH BEANS WITH FERMENTED BEAN CURD

China

Imperial (Metric)	American
1 pound (455g) French beans	3 cups French beans
¼ pint (150ml) vegetable stock	⅔ cup vegetable stock
4 tablespoons groundnut oil	4 tablespoons peanut oil
1 garlic clove, finely chopped	1 garlic clove, finely chopped
1 tablespoon mashed, fermented bean curd	1 tablespoon mashed, fermented bean curd
2 tablespoons tamari or shoyu sauce	2 tablespoons tamari or shoyu sauce

1

Top and tail the beans. Bring the stock to a boil in a saucepan. Put in the beans, cover, and simmer 15 minutes, or until they are just tender. Drain.

2

Heat the oil in a wok or large frying pan over a high heat. Put in the beans and garlic, and stir-fry 1 minute.

3

Mix in the fermented bean curd and tamari or shoyu sauce. Stir-fry 1 minute more, and remove the pan from the heat.

Note: Not suitable for freezing.

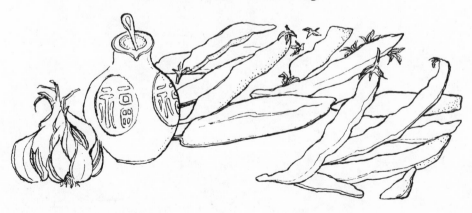

STIR-FRIED MANGETOUT (SNOW PEAS) WITH WATER CHESTNUTS

China

Imperial (Metric)	American
1 pound (455g) mangetout peas	1 pound snow peas
One 8 ounce (225g) tin water chestnuts	2 cups water chestnuts
2 garlic cloves, peeled and left whole	2 garlic cloves, peeled and left whole
4 tablespoons Chinese rice wine or dry sherry	4 tablespoons Chinese rice wine or dry sherry
2 tablespoons tamari or shoyu sauce	2 tablespoons tamari or shoyu sauce

1

Top and tail the peas. Drain and thinly slice the water chestnuts.

2

Heat the oil in a wok or large frying pan over high heat. Put in the peas, water chestnuts and garlic, and stir-fry 2 minutes. Remove the garlic.

3

Pour in the wine or sherry and tamari or shoyu sauce. Lower the heat and stir-fry a further 2 minutes.

Note: Not suitable for freezing.

STIR-FRIED BEAN SPROUTS WITH GREEN PEPPERS

China

Imperial (Metric)	American
12 ounces (340g) bean sprouts	6 cups bean sprouts
3 green peppers	3 sweet green peppers
4 tablespoons groundnut oil	4 tablespoons peanut oil
1 garlic clove, finely chopped	1 garlic clove, finely chopped
½ ounce (15g) fresh ginger root, peeled and grated	½ ounce fresh ginger, peeled and grated
2 tablespoons Chinese rice wine or dry sherry	2 tablespoons Chinese rice wine or dry sherry
2 tablespoons tamari or shoyu sauce	2 tablespoons tamari or shoyu sauce

1

Core and seed the peppers, and cut them into 1-inch (2.5 cm) squares.

2

Heat the oil in a wok or large frying pan over high heat. Put in the garlic and ginger, and stir-fry 30 seconds.

3

Put in the peppers, and stir-fry 1 minute. Mix in the bean sprouts, and stir-fry a further 1 minute.

4

Add the wine or sherry and tamari or shoyu sauce, and stir-fry 1 minute more. The vegetables should both still be crisp.

Note: Not suitable for freezing.

STIR-FRIED SPINACH WITH BAMBOO SHOOTS

China

Imperial (Metric)	American
1 pound (455g) spinach	4 cups spinach
One 8-ounce (225g) tin bamboo shoots	2 cups bamboo shoots
4 tablespoons oil	¼ cup oil
2 tablespoons tamari or shoyu sauce	2 tablespoons tamari or shoyu sauce
2 tablespoons Chinese rice wine or dry sherry	2 tablespoons Chinese rice wine or dry sherry

1

Tear away the stems of the spinach. Thinly slice the bamboo shoots.

2

In a wok or large frying pan, heat the oil over high heat. Put in the bamboo shoots. Stir-fry ½ minute and remove.

3

Put in the spinach. Stir-fry 2 minutes. Add the sauce and sherry, and stir-fry ½ minute more.

4

Replace the bamboo shoots. Continue cooking ¼ minute. The vegetables should both still be crisp.

Note: Not suitable for freezing.

THE TWO WINTERS

China

Imperial (Metric)	American
1 ounce (25g) Chinese dried mushrooms	1 oz Chinese dried mushrooms
One 8 ounce (225g) tin bamboo shoots	2 cups bamboo shoots
1 teaspoon arrowroot	1 teaspoon arrowroot
3 tablespoons groundnut oil	3 tablespoons peanut oil
2 tablespoons tamari or shoyu sauce	2 tablespoons tamari or shoyu sauce
½ tablespoon sesame oil	½ tablespoon sesame oil

1

Soak the mushrooms in warm water to cover for 30 minutes. Drain them reserving the water. Halve.

2

Thinly slice the bamboo shoots.

3

Put the arrowroot in a bowl, and gradually mix in 4 tablespoons of the mushroom water.

4

Heat the oil in a wok or large frying pan over high heat. Put in the mushrooms and bamboo shoots, and stir-fry 1 minute. Add the tamari or shoyu sauce, and stir-fry 2 minutes.

5

Pour in the arrowroot mixture, and stir until the liquid thickens slightly.

6

Add the sesame oil, and take the pan from the heat.

Note: To freeze, cool completely and pack into lidded containers. Store for up to 2 months. Thaw at room temperature, and reheat by quickly stirring the mixture over high heat in a wok or large frying pan.

STIR-BRAISED MIXED VEGETABLES

China

Imperial (Metric)	American
8 ounces (225g) broccoli	1½ cups broccoli florets
8 ounces (225g) carrots	2 to 3 small carrots
4 celery sticks	4 celery stalks
4 spring onions	4 scallions
3 tablespoons groundnut oil	3 tablespoons peanut oil
3 fl ounces (90ml) vegetable stock	⅓ cup vegetable stock
2 tablespoons Chinese rice wine or dry sherry	2 tablespoons Chinese rice wine or dry sherry
2 tablespoons tamari or shoyu sauce	2 tablespoons tamari or shoyu sauce

1

Cut the broccoli into small florettes.

2

Cut the carrots into thin, diagonal slices.

3

Cut the celery sticks into 1-inch (2.5 cm) squares. Cut the onions into 1-inch (2.5 cm) lengths.

4

Heat the oil in a wok or large frying pan over high heat. Put in all the vegetables, and stir-fry 2 minutes.

5

Pour in the stock, wine or sherry and tamari or shoyu sauce. Bring to a boil.

6

Cover the pan tightly, and cook over medium heat 10 minutes. The vegetables should be just tender and all the liquid evaporated.

Note: Not suitable for freezing.

SPICY BEAN SPROUT SALAD

China

Imperial (Metric)	American
1 pound (455g) bean sprouts	8 cups bean sprouts
4 spring onions	4 scallions
4 tablespoons sesame oil	4 tablespoons sesame oil
2 tablespoons tamari or shoyu sauce	2 tablespoons tamari or shoyu sauce
1 tablespoon white wine vinegar	1 tablespoon white wine vinegar
$\frac{1}{4}$ teaspoon chilli sauce	$\frac{1}{4}$ teaspoon chili sauce
1 garlic clove, crushed	1 garlic clove, crushed
2 tablespoons chopped, fresh coriander or parsley	2 tablespoons chopped, fresh cilantro or parsley

1

Bring a pan of water to a boil. Put in the bean sprouts, and cook for 30 seconds. Drain, and run cold water through them. Drain again.

2

Cut the onions into 1-inch (2.5 cm) lengths. Mix into the bean sprouts.

3

Beat together the remaining ingredients. Fold the resulting dressing into the bean sprouts and onions.

4

Put the salad on a serving plate, and scatter the coriander (cilantro) or parsley over the top.

Note: Not suitable for freezing.

COLD, SLICED LOTUS ROOT

China

Imperial (Metric)	American
One 1 pound (455g) tin lotus root	One 1 pound can lotus root
2 fresh or 4 dried chillies	2 fresh or 4 dried red chilis
2 tablespoons groundnut oil	2 tablespoons peanut oil
1 tablespoon sesame oil	1 tablespoon sesame oil
2 tablespoons white wine vinegar	2 tablespoons white wine vinegar
2 tablespoons tamari or shoyu sauce	2 tablespoons tamari or shoyu sauce

1
Thinly slice the lotus root.

2
Thinly slice the fresh chillies with their seeds. Tear the dried chillies into several pieces.

3
Heat the oil in a wok or frying pan over medium heat. Put in the chillies and fry them, stirring frequently, for 2 minutes. Strain the oil into a bowl.

4
Add the sesame oil, wine vinegar and tamari or shoyu sauce.

5
Turn the lotus root in the mixture, and let stand for 15 minutes before serving.

Note: Not suitable for freezing.

SWEET AND SOUR RADISH SALAD

China

Imperial (Metric)	American
32 radishes	32 radishes
3 tablespoons white wine vinegar	3 tablespoons white wine vinegar
3 tablespoons tamari or shoyu sauce	3 tablespoons tamari or shoyu sauce
1 teaspoon Barbados sugar	1 teaspoon brown sugar
1 teaspoon sesame oil	1 teaspoon sesame oil

1

Top and tail the radishes. Crush each one by banging it with a hammer or cleaver. Put them in a bowl.

2

Mix together the vinegar, tamari or shoyu sauce and sugar.

3

Fold the mixture into the radishes. Put the radishes in the refrigerator for 2 hours.

4

Stir in the sesame oil just before serving.

Note: Not suitable for freezing.

RED-COOKED CABBAGE

China

Imperial (Metric)	American
1 firmly packed green cabbage	1 firmly packed green cabbage
6 spring onions	6 scallions
4 tablespoons stock	¼ cup stock
3 tablespoons soy sauce	3 tablespoons soy sauce
3 tablespoons oil	3 tablespoons oil
1 garlic clove, finely chopped	1 garlic clove, finely chopped
1 ounce (25g) fresh ginger root, peeled	1 ounce fresh ginger, peeled
Pinch of Szechuan pepper	Pinch of Szechuan pepper

1

Shred the cabbage. Chop the spring onions (scallions) into 1-inch (2.5 cm) lengths. Mix together the stock and soy sauce.

2

Heat the oil in a wok or large heavy frying pan over high heat.

3

Put in the garlic, and grate in the ginger. Put in the cabbage, and stir-fry 1 minute.

4

Pour in the stock and sauce mixture, and bring to a boil. Add the pepper.

5

Cover and cook over low heat for 10 minutes so the cabbage is just tender.

Note: Not suitable for freezing.

SPINACH WITH TOASTED SESAME SEEDS

Japan

Imperial (Metric)	American
1½ pounds (675g) spinach	6 cups spinach
Pinch of sea salt	Pinch of sea salt
3 tablespoons kombu stock (page 18)	3 tablespoons kombu stock (page 18)
2 tablespoons tamari or shoyu sauce	2 tablespoons tamari or shoyu sauce
2 tablespoons sesame seeds	2 tablespoons sesame seeds

1

Bring 12 fl ounces (340ml or 1½ cups) water to a boil in a large saucepan. Add the sea salt. Gather the spinach into a large bunch and put it in the pan, stalk side down. Cover and cook for 5 minutes or until the upper leaves begin to wilt. Drain the spinach, and plunge it into cold water. Drain again.

2

Cut away and discard the stalks with a sharp knife. Squeeze the leaves as dry as possible. Cut the leaves into 1-inch (2.5 cm) pieces, and squeeze them dry again. Put in a large bowl.

3

Mix together the kombu stock and tamari or shoyu sauce. Fold the mixture into the spinach.

4

Heat a heavy frying pan over a moderate heat without any fat. Put in the sesame seeds and stir around until they brown and begin to jump. Turn them on to a plate to cool.

5

Divide the spinach among four small bowls. Scatter the sesame seeds over the top.

Note: Not suitable for freezing.

CHILLI CABBAGE WITH COCONUT

Malaysia

Imperial (Metric)	American
1 green cabbage	1 green cabbage
1 medium onion	1 medium onion
3 green chillies	3 green chilis
3 fl ounces (90ml) water	⅓ cup water
2 tablespoons desiccated coconut	2 tablespoons dried coconut
¼ teaspoon ground turmeric	¼ teaspoon ground turmeric

1

Shred the cabbage. Thinly slice the onion. Halve the chillies lengthways. Core and seed them. Cut them into thin, crossways slices.

2

Mix together the coconut and turmeric.

3

Put the cabbage, onion, chillies and water in a saucepan. Cover, and set over high heat. Cook 10 minutes, stirring half way through.

4

Add the coconut and turmeric mixture, and stir until there is a strong smell of coconut, about 1 minute. Take the pan from the heat, and serve as soon as possible.

Note: Not suitable for freezing.

TEMPURA

Japan

Imperial (Metric)	American
4 ounces (115g) French beans	¾ cup French beans
6 ounces (170g) carrots	2 small carrots
One 8-ounce (225g) tin bamboo shoots in large pieces, not sliced	2 cups bamboo shoots in large pieces, not sliced
12 mangetout peas	12 snow peas
12 asparagus stalks	12 asparagus stalks
12 fresh button mushrooms	12 fresh button mushrooms
Batter:	**Batter:**
1 egg yolk	1 egg yolk
Pinch of bicarbonate of soda	Pinch of baking soda
¾ pint (425ml) iced water	2 cups ice water
7 ounces (200g) wholewheat flour	1¾ cups whole wheat flour
Dipping Sauce:	**Dipping Sauce:**
3 fl ounces (90ml) sake or dry sherry	⅓ cup sake or dry sherry
¼ pint (140ml) tamari or shoyu sauce	⅔ cup tamari or shoyu sauce
8 fl ounces (225ml) kombu stock	1 cup kombu stock
2 tablespoons flaked, dried bonito or crumbled nori	2 tablespoons flaked, dried bonito or crumbled nori
Sesame Dipping Sauce:	**Sesame Dipping Sauce:**
1 tablespoon tahini	1 tablespoon tahini
3 tablespoons sake or dry sherry	3 tablespoons sake or dry sherry
4 tablespoons tamari or shoyu sauce	4 tablespoons tamari or shoyu sauce
Garnish:	**Garnish:**
2 lemons, thinly sliced	2 lemons, thinly sliced
Sea salt	Sea salt

1

Make the sauces. Heat the sake or sherry in a saucepan over moderate heat until lukewarm. Ignite it, and shake the pan gently until the flame dies. Add half the tamari or shoyu sauce, the kombu stock and dried bonito. Bring them to a boil, and strain through a sieve. Cool completely, and add the remaining tamari or shoyu sauce. For the sesame dipping sauce, put the tahini in a bowl and gradually beat in the remaining ingredients.

Continued over

2

Top and tail the beans. Blanch in boiling water for 2 minutes. Drain.

3

Cut the carrots into thin, diagonal slices.

4

Quarter the pieces of bamboo shoot so they are in fingers about ½-inch (1.5 cm) thick.

5

Cut 4-inch (10 cm) tips from the asparagus stalks. Discard the rest.

6

Trim the stalks of the mushrooms to about ½ inch (1.5 cm).

7

Make the batter. Lightly beat the egg yolk in a bowl. Beat in the bicarbonate of soda (baking soda) and then the water. Scatter in the flour, and mix well with a wooden spoon. Keep the batter standing for no longer than 10 minutes once it is made.

8

Heat the oven to 250F/130C/gas ½. This is to keep the vegetables warm once they are cooked. Heat a pan of deep oil to 375F/190C.

9

Work with one type of vegetable at a time. Using chopsticks or tongs, dip each piece separately into the batter. Deep-fry the pieces, about 6 at a time, for 2 minutes. turning them once. They should have a crisp, golden-brown coating. Lift them out of the oil and put them into dishes or baskets lined with paper towels. Put them in the oven to keep warm while you cook the other types of vegetables in the same way.

10

To serve, arrange a selection of the vegetables on each of four plates. Give each person a small bowl of dipping sauce and, on a small plate, thin slices of lemon arranged around a small pile of sea salt. The lemon slices should be squeezed over the vegetables which can then be dipped in the sauce or salt as wished.

Note: Tempura is usually served as part of a main meal. To make it more substantial, up to 12 oz (340 g or ¾ pound) bean curd can be cut into ¼-inch (6 mm) slices, dipped in batter and fried in the same way as the vegetables.

Note: Not suitable for freezing.

SWEETCORN PANCAKES

Indonesia

Imperial (Metric)	*American*
One 12-ounce (370g) tin sweetcorn kernels	1½ cups sweet corn kernels
1 small onion, finely chopped	1 small onion, finely chopped
1 garlic clove, bruised and finely chopped	1 garlic clove, bruised and finely chopped
2 tablespoons finely chopped celery	2 tablespoons finely chopped celery
2 green or red chillies, cored, seeded and finely chopped	2 green or red chilies, cored, seeded and finely chopped
Pinch of sea salt	Pinch of sea salt
Freshly ground black pepper	Freshly ground black pepper
1 egg, beaten	1 egg, beaten
2 tablespoons wholewheat flour	2 tablespoons whole wheat flour
Pinch of bicarbonate of soda	Pinch of baking soda
4 tablespoons water	4 tablespoons water
Oil for greasing	Oil for greasing

1

Mix all the ingredients together.

2

Lightly oil a heavy frying pan. Heat it over high heat. Put 1 tablespoon amounts in the pan, about three at a time. Cook until the underside is brown and the mixture is set. Turn them over to brown the other side. Lift the pancakes out, and keep them warm.

3

Cook the remaining mixture in the same way, regreasing the pan as and when necessary.

Note: Not suitable for freezing.

TOSSED SALAD

China

Imperial (Metric)	American
1 large cos lettuce	1 large cos lettuce
8 ounces (225g) carrots	2 to 3 small carrots
4 ounces (115g) bean sprouts	2 cups bean sprouts
1 medium onion	1 medium onion
3 tablespoons groundnut oil	3 tablespoons peanut oil
1 garlic clove, crushed	1 garlic clove, crushed
½ ounce (15g) fresh ginger root, peeled and grated	½ ounce fresh ginger root, peeled and grated
2 tablespoons vegetable stock	2 tablespoons vegetable stock
2 tablespoons tamari or shoyu sauce	2 tablespoons tamari or shoyu sauce
1 tablespoon hoisin sauce	1 tablespoon hoisin sauce
1½ tablespoons Chinese rice wine or dry sherry	1½ tablespoons Chinese rice wine or dry sherry
1 tablespoon sesame oil	1 tablespoon sesame oil

1

Cut the lettuce leaves into pieces 1 by 2 inches (2.5 by 5 cm). Cut the carrots into matchstick pieces.

2

Finely chop the onion.

3

Heat the oil in a frying pan over high heat. Put in the onion, garlic and ginger, and stir-fry for 1 minute. Add the vegetable stock, bring it to a boil, and take the pan off the heat.

4

Mix in the tamari or shoyu sauce, hoisin sauce, wine or sherry and sesame oil.

5

Put the lettuce, carrots and bean sprouts in a bowl. Pour the dressing over them, and toss to coat.

Note: Not suitable for freezing.

DAIKON (WHITE RADISH) AND CARROT IN VINEGAR DRESSING

Japan

Imperial (Metric)	American
8 ounces (225g) white radish	1½ cups white radish, grated
8 ounces (225g) carrots	2 to 3 small carrots
1 teaspoon sea salt	1 teaspoon sea salt
7 fl ounces (200ml) cold water	¾ cup cold water
¼ ounce (10g) flaked dried bonito or nori sheet	¼ ounce flaked dried bonito or nori sheet
1 tablespoon white wine vinegar	1 tablespoon white wine vinegar
1 teaspoon Barbados sugar	1 teaspoon brown sugar

1

Finely grate the white radish and carrots. Put them in a bowl, sprinkle with salt, and add the water. Let soak for 30 minutes.

2

If you are using nori instead of bonito, crumble it. Put the nori or bonito in a small frying pan. Cook, stirring, over low heat for 3 minutes so the colour brightens. Crumble it finely or grind it to a powder in a coffee grinder.

3

Drain the white radish and carrot. Squeeze as much water from them as possible. Put them into a mixing bowl. Stir in the vinegar and sugar and then the powdered seaweed.

4

Serve in small bowls either as a first course or as a salad side dish.

Note: Not suitable for freezing.

FRENCH BEANS WITH SOY AND SESAME DRESSING

Japan

Imperial (Metric)	American
1 pound (455g) French beans	1 pound French beans
4 fl ounces (125ml) kombu stock	½ cup kombu stock
1 teaspoon Barbados sugar	1 teaspoon brown sugar
1 tablespoon sake or dry sherry	1 tablespoon sake or dry sherry
1 teaspoon tamari or shoyu sauce	1 teaspoon tamari or shoyu sauce
Dressing.	Dressing:
3 tablespoons sake or dry sherry	3 tablespoons sake or dry sherry
1 tablespoon tahini (sesame paste)	1 tablespoon tahini (sesame paste)
2 tablespoons tamari or shoyu sauce	2 tablespoons tamari or shoyu sauce

1

Top and tail the beans. Cut into ½-inch (1.5 cm) lengths. Bring a pan of water to a boil. Put in the beans and cook for 8 minutes or until just tender. Drain, and run cold water through them.

2

Put the kombu stock, sugar, sake or sherry and tamari or shoyu sauce in a saucepan, and bring to a boil. Put in the beans and return them to a boil. Take the pan from the heat, and cool the beans to room temperature in the liquid.

3

For the dressing, heat the sake gently in a saucepan. Take the pan from the heat. Ignite the sake, and shake the pan until the flame dies. Cool the sake to room temperature.

4

Put the tahini in a bowl, and gradually beat in the sake and the tamari or shoyu sauce.

5

Drain the beans, and put them in a bowl. Mix in the dressing.

Note: This can be served as a first course or as a salad to accompany a Japanese meal. Not suitable for freezing.

CELERY AND CUCUMBER HOT SALAD

China

Imperial (Metric)	American
1 head celery	1 head celery
1 medium cucumber	1 medium cucumber
8 ounces (225g) beetroot (raw)	1 cup beets (raw)
2 tablespoons tamari or shoyu sauce	2 tablespoons tamari or shoyu sauce
1 tablespoon plum sauce (or hoisin if none is available)	1 tablespoon plum sauce (or hoisin if none is available)
1 tablespoon white wine vinegar	1 tablespoon white wine vinegar
1 tablespoon Chinese rice wine or dry sherry	1 tablespoon Chinese rice wine or dry sherry
1 teaspoon chilli sauce	1 teaspoon chili sauce
3 tablespoons groundnut oil	3 tablespoons peanut oil
1 tablespoon sesame oil	1 tablespoon sesame oil

1

Cut the celery, cucumber and beetroot (beets) into matchstick pieces.

2

Mix together the tamari or shoyu sauce, plum sauce, vinegar, wine or sherry and chilli sauce.

3

Heat the oil in a wok or large saucepan over high heat. Put in the vegetables, and stir-fry 1 minute.

4

Add the flavouring mixture, and stir-fry a further 1 minute.

5

Take the pan from the heat. Mix in the sesame oil. Serve immediately.

Note: Not suitable for freezing.

PEPPER AND BAMBOO SHOOT HOT SALAD

China

Imperial (Metric)	American
2 red peppers	1 sweet red pepper
2 green peppers	2 sweet green peppers
One 8-ounce (225g) tin bamboo shoots	2 cups bamboo shoots
2 tablespoons tamari or shoyu sauce	2 tablespoons tamari or shoyu sauce
1 tablespoon hoisin sauce	1 tablespoon hoisin sauce
2 tablespoons Chinese rice wine or dry sherry	2 tablespoons Chinese rice wine or dry sherry
2 teaspoons chilli sauce	2 teaspoons chili sauce
3 tablespoons groundnut oil	3 tablespoons peanut oil

1

Core and seed the peppers, and cut them into 1-inch (2.5 cm) squares. Thinly slice the bamboo shoots.

2

Mix together the tamari or shoyu sauce, hoisin sauce, wine or sherry and chilli sauce.

3

Heat the oil in a wok or large frying pan over high heat. Put in the peppers and bamboo shoots, and stir-fry $\frac{1}{2}$ minute.

4

Put in the mixture of flavouring ingredients, and stir-fry a further $\frac{1}{2}$ minute.

5

Take the pan from the heat, and serve as soon as possible.

Note: Not suitable for freezing.

SZECHUAN PICKLED VEGETABLES

China

Imperial (Metric)	American
6 fresh, red chillies	6 fresh, red chilis
4 tablespoons sea salt	4 tablespoons sea salt
2 tablespoons Szechuan peppercorns	2 tablespoons Szechuan peppercorns
3 pints (1.8 litres) boiling water	8 cups boiling water
1 tablespoon Barbados sugar	1 tablespoon brown sugar
2 tablespoons Chinese rice wine or dry sherry	2 tablespoons Chinese rice wine or dry sherry
1 ounce (25g) fresh ginger root, sliced	1 ounce fresh ginger, sliced
2 garlic cloves, bruised	2 garlic cloves, bruised
8 ounces (225g) carrots	3 small carrots
8 ounces (225g) white turnips	1 to 2 medium, white turnips
1 medium cucumber	1 medium cucumber
8 ounces (225g) green cabbage	2 cups green cabbage, cut in squares

1

Core and seed the chillies, and cut them into thin strips.

2

Put the salt and pepper in a frying pan. Set over medium heat, and stir for 2 minutes, or until they smell highly aromatic. Take the pan from the heat.

3

Put the boiling water in a large bowl or crock. Stir in the salt and pepper mixture, sugar, wine or sherry, ginger root, garlic and chillies. Let the liquid stand for 2 hours.

4

Cut the carrots, turnips and cucumber into pieces about 1½ inches by ¾ inch (4 by 2 cm). Cut the cabbage into 2-inch (5 cm) squares.

5

Put the vegetables in the liquid. Cover tightly, and refrigerate for 3 days before serving.

Note: These pickles should be served cold with a hot main dish, in a similar way to a salad.

VEGETABLE CURRY WITH YOGURT

Malabar

Imperial (Metric)	American
8 ounces (225g) potatoes	1 to 2 medium potatoes
6 ounces (170g) carrots	2 small carrots
6 ounces (170g) okra or French beans	1 cup okra or French beans
6 ounces (170g) shelled green peas, (fresh or frozen)	1 cup shelled green peas, (fresh or frozen)
4 green chillies	4 green chilis
½ pint (285ml) water	1⅓ cups water
Pinch of sea salt	Pinch of sea salt
Pinch of turmeric	Pinch of turmeric
½ fresh coconut, grated	½ fresh coconut, grated
8 fl ounces (225ml) natural yogurt	1 cup plain yogurt

1

Peel and dice the potatoes. Cut the carrots into diagonal slices. Trim the tops from the okra or top and tail the beans, and cut them into 1-inch (2.5 cm) lengths. Core, seed and chop the chillies.

2

Put the water in a saucepan, and bring to a boil. Put in all the vegetables plus the salt and turmeric. Cover and simmer for 20 minutes, or until the vegetables are tender and most of the water has been absorbed.

3

Mix the coconut into the yogurt.

4

Take the pan from the heat. Mix in the coconut and yogurt. Bring the vegetables back to just below boiling point before serving.

Note: Not suitable for freezing.

AUBERGINE (EGGPLANT) CURRY

Malaysia

Imperial (Metric)	American
2 medium aubergines	2 medium eggplant
1 tablespoon sea salt	1 tablespoon sea salt
2 medium onions	2 medium onions
4 green chillies	4 green chilis
1 garlic clove, crushed	1 garlic clove, crushed
½ teaspoon fenugreek seeds, crushed	½ teaspooon fenugreek seeds, crushed
1 teaspoon ground turmeric	1 teaspoon ground turmeric
12 fl ounces (340ml) thick coconut milk	1½ cups thick coconut milk
Pinch of sea salt	Pinch of sea salt

1

Cut the aubergines (eggplant) into ¾-inch (2 cm) dice. Put them in a colander, and sprinkle with the 1 tablespoon salt. Leave to drain for 20 minutes. Rinse with cold water, and dry with paper towels.

2

Finely chop the onions. Slice the chillies into rounds without removing their seeds.

3

Put the onions, chillies, garlic, fenugreek and turmeric in a saucepan. Put the aubergine (eggplant) pieces on top. Pour in the coconut milk, and add the salt.

4

Bring gently to a boil. Cover, and cook over low heat for 10 minutes. Stir and cook for 10 minutes more or until the aubergines (eggplant) are soft.

Note: Not suitable for freezing.

MIXED, PICKLED VEGETABLES

Indonesia

These are served as a hot or cold side dish rather than as a pickle.

Imperial (Metric)	American
1 green pepper	1 sweet green pepper
4 ounces (115g) cabbage	1 cup cabbage, shredded
4 ounces (115g) carrots	1 medium carrot
3 ounces (85g) cauliflower	$\frac{1}{3}$ cup cauliflower
$\frac{1}{2}$ small cucumber	$\frac{1}{2}$ small cucumber
2 red or green chillies	2 red or green chilis
$\frac{1}{2}$ ounce (15g) fresh ginger root	$\frac{1}{2}$ ounce fresh ginger
2 medium onions	2 medium onions
1 garlic clove, chopped	1 garlic clove, chopped
$\frac{1}{2}$ teaspoon ground turmeric	$\frac{1}{2}$ teaspoon ground turmeric
4 macadamia nuts or blanched almonds	4 macadamia nuts or blanched almonds
3 tablespoons groundnut oil	3 tablespoons peanut oil
2 teaspoons Barbados sugar	2 teaspoons brown sugar
1 stalk lemon grass, bruised	1 stalk lemon grass, bruised
3 tablespoons white wine vinegar	3 tablespoons white wine vinegar

1

Core and seed the pepper, and cut it into pieces 1 inch by $\frac{1}{4}$ inch (2.5 cm by 6 mm).

2

Shred the cabbage. Cut the carrots into matchstick pieces. Cut the cauliflower into small florettes. Peel the cucumber. Cut it into lengthways quarters, and cut away the seeds. Cut the rest into matchstick pieces.

3

Cut each chilli into lengthways quarters. Core and seed them. Peel and thinly slice the ginger root. Thinly slice the onions.

4

Crush the garlic, and mash it with the turmeric to make a paste. Crush the nuts, and mix them into the paste.

114

5

Heat the oil in a wok or large frying pan over medium heat. Put in the onion slices, and stir-fry until golden. Add the paste, and stir for 2 minutes.

6

Put in the chillies, sugar, lemon grass and vinegar. Add 8 fl ounces (225ml or 2 cups) water, and bring everything to a boil.

7

Put in the vegetables. Simmer, uncovered, for 5 minutes, stirring frequently.

Note: Not suitable for freezing.

CHILLI-SIMMERED VEGETABLES

Sumatra

Imperial (Metric)	American
6 ounces (170g) green cabbage	1½ cups green cabbage, shredded
6 ounces (170g) French beans	¾ cup French beans
6 ounces (170g) potatoes	1 medium potato
2 tomatoes	2 tomatoes
1 to 2 teaspoons chilli powder, according to taste	1 to 2 teaspoons chili powder, according to taste
2 medium onions, finely chopped	2 medium onions, finely chopped
3 garlic cloves, crushed	3 garlic cloves, crushed
1 teaspoon Laos powder	1 teaspoon Laos powder
2 tablespoons groundnut oil	2 tablespoons peanut oil
Pinch of sea salt	Pinch of sea salt
¾ pint (425ml) thick coconut milk	2 cups thick coconut milk
3 curry leaves	3 curry leaves

1

Shred the cabbage. Top and tail the beans, and cut them into 1½-inch (4 cm) lengths. Peel the potatoes, and cut them into ¾-inch (2 cm) dice. Scald, skin and finely chop the tomatoes.

2

Put the chilli powder, onions, garlic, Laos powder and oil in a blender. Work to a smooth paste.

3

Put the paste in a wok or large frying pan. Set over medium heat and sauté it, stirring continually, until it is brown and smells highly aromatic.

4

Add the tomatoes, and stir 1 minute.

5

Pour in the coconut milk, add the curry leaves and bring to a boil.

6

Put in the vegetables. Simmer, uncovered, for 25 minutes, or until the potatoes are just tender.

Note: Not suitable for freezing.

Chapter 6
Rice

Rice is the staple food all over the eastern world. It is served as an accompaniment to nearly every meal, it is ground to make flour and noodles and fermented to make wine.

In Japan the amount of rice that was harvested by the ruling lords once determined their rank. Their word for meal is 'gohan', which also means rice.

In Indonesia rice is eaten three times a day. Breakfast may consist of last night's leftovers, fried, or it could be freshly cooked and topped with fresh papayas and coconut milk. Lunch consists of rice, with one or perhaps two vegetable or meat dishes. Rice cakes are served at tea time with fried bananas, and supper, the largest meal, brings rice again, accompanied by up to four savoury dishes.

In all eastern countries the eating of white rice has always been a symbol of high status, exactly as eating white bread has been in Europe. Although health consciousness is awakening in the East, all the recipe books at present call for white rice. In most cases, you can simply substitute brown, but remember to account for the longer cooking time.

The glutinous or sticky rice that is so popular in Laos and is used for the porridgy Chinese dish known as Congee has at present no readily available substitute. For Congee I have used short-grain brown rice and have cut down on the amount of liquid used. It will not, however, be as smooth and sticky as it would be if made with glutinous rice. The final effect is, however, very similar to the original, and if you enjoy brown rice you will find the flavour better.

BOILED RICE

China

Imperial (Metric)	American
8 ounces (225g) long-grain brown rice	1 cup long-grain brown rice
1 pint (570ml) water	2½ cups water
Pinch of sea salt	Pinch of sea salt

1

Put the rice, water and salt in a heavy saucepan. Bring to a boil.

2

Cover, and cook gently for 40 to 45 minutes or until all the water has been absorbed.

3

Take the pan from the heat, and let the rice stand, still covered, a further 10 minutes.

Note: This method works bests if you do not lift the lid while the rice is cooking. To freeze, cool completely, pack into plastic containers and cover. Store for up to two months. Thaw at room temperature. Reheat by either tossing in a little oil in a saucepan or by stir-frying in a wok or frying pan. Or use cold to make one of the fried rice dishes or salads that follow.

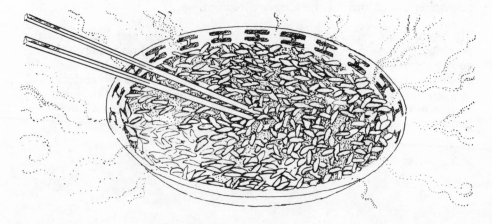

VEGETABLE RICE

China

Imperial (Metric)	American
8 ounces (225g) long-grain brown rice	1 cup long-grain brown rice
12 ounces (340g) vegetables, for example,	3 cups vegetables, for example,
12 ounces (340g) spring greens or spinach chopped	3 cups spring greens or spinach, chopped
8 ounces (225g) bamboo shoots sliced, plus	1 cup bamboo shoots sliced, plus ¾ cup mushrooms, sliced
4 ounces (115g) mushrooms, sliced	¾ cup each diced carrots, cucumber and chopped watercress
4 ounces (115g) each diced carrots, cucumber and chopped watercress	1⅓ cup green peas and ¾ cup sliced mushrooms
8 ounces (225g) green peas and 4 ounces (115g) sliced mushrooms	2½ cups water
1 pint (570ml) water	Pinch of sea salt or 1 tablespoon tamari or shoyu sauce
Pinch of sea salt or 1 tablespoon tamari or shoyu sauce	

1

Mix the rice and vegetables in a heavy saucepan. Add the water and salt or tamari or shoyu sauce.

2

Cook as for Boiled Rice (left-hand page).

Note: Not suitable for freezing.

FRIED RICE

China

Imperial (Metric)	American
8 ounces (225g) long-grain brown rice	1 cup long-grain brown rice
1 pint (570ml) water	2½ cups water
Pinch of sea salt	Pinch of sea salt
2 eggs	2 eggs
2 tablespoons tamari or shoyu sauce	2 tablespoons tamari or shoyu sauce
3 tablespoons groundnut oil	3 tablespoons peanut oil

1

Cook the rice with the water and salt as for Boiled Rice. Tip it into a flat dish, and let it cool and dry.

2

Beat the eggs with the tamari or shoyu sauce.

3

Heat the oil in a wok or large frying pan over medium heat. Pour in the eggs, and stir until they just begin to set.

4

Mix in the rice, and stir about 2 minutes so it heats through and becomes coated with the egg.

Note: Not suitable for freezing.

FRIED RICE WITH SPRING ONIONS (SCALLIONS) AND BAMBOO SHOOTS

China

Imperial (Metric)	American
8 ounces (225g) long-grain brown rice	1 cup long-grain brown rice
1 pint (570ml) water	2½ cups water
Pinch of sea salt	Pinch of sea salt
2 eggs	2 eggs
2 tablespoons tamari or shoyu sauce	2 tablespoons tamari or shoyu sauce
8 spring onions	8 scallions
6 ounces (175g) drained, tinned bamboo shoots	1½ cups drained, canned bamboo shoots
4 tablespoons groundnut oil	4 tablespoons peanut oil
2 tablespoons Chinese pickled vegetables	2 tablespoons Chinese pickled vegetables

1

Cook the rice as for Boiled Rice (page 118). Tip it into a flat dish, and let it cool and dry. Beat the eggs with the tamari or shoyu sauce.

2

Cut the spring onions (scallions) into 1-inch (2.5 cm) lengths. Thinly slice the bamboo shoots.

3

Heat the oil in a wok or large frying pan over high heat. Put in the spring onions (scallions) and bamboo shoots. Stir-fry for 1 minute and then remove.

4

Lower the heat to medium. Put in the egg, and stir until it is just beginning to set.

5

Mix in the rice, and stir for 1 minute. Add the onions, bamboo shoots and pickles, and continue to stir for a further minute.

Note: Not suitable for freezing.

121

FRIED RICE WITH PEAS, MUSHROOMS AND SHREDDED EGG

China

Imperial (Metric)	American
8 ounces (225g) long-grain brown rice	1 cup long-grain brown rice
1 pint (570ml) water	2½ cups water
Pinch of sea salt	Pinch of sea salt
4 ounces (115g) mushrooms	¾ cup mushrooms
3 fl ounces (90ml) groundnut oil	⅓ cup peanut oil
2 eggs, beaten	2 eggs, beaten
4 ounces (115g) cooked, green peas	⅔ cup cooked, green peas
2 tablespoons tamari or shoyu sauce	2 tablespoons tamari or shoyu sauce

1

Cook the rice as for Boiled Rice (page 118). Tip it into a flat dish to cool and dry.

2

Thinly slice the mushrooms. Heat 2 tablespoons of the oil in a wok or frying pan over high heat. Put in the mushrooms, and stir-fry 1 minute. Remove.

3

In another wok or large frying pan, heat 2 tablespoons oil over high heat. Pour in the eggs, and cook until they set into a flat omelette. Lift it out, and cut it into shreds.

.4

Add the remaining oil to the original pan. Set it over high heat. Put in the rice, peas and mushrooms, and stir-fry 1 minute or until heated through.

5

Mix in the tamari or shoyu sauce and half the shredded egg. Take the pan from the heat.

6

Put the rice into a serving dish, and scatter the remaining egg over the top.

Note: Not suitable for freezing.

FRUITY RICE SALAD

China

Imperial (Metric)	American
8 ounces (225g) long-grain brown rice	1 cup long-grain brown rice
¼ large cucumber	¼ large cucumber
3 ounces (85g) beetroot, cooked	3 small beets, cooked
4 ounces (115g) green grapes	½ cup green grapes
2 medium oranges or 4 tangerines or satsumas	2 medium oranges or 4 tangerines or satsumas
2 tablespoons tamari or shoyu sauce	2 tablespoons tamari or shoyu sauce
2 tablespoons Chinese rice wine or dry sherry	2 tablespoons Chinese rice wine or dry sherry
4 tablespoons groundnut oil	4 tablespoons peanut oil
3 ounces (85g) raisins	½ cup raisins

1

Boil the rice as for Boiled Rice (page 118). Tip it on to a plate to cool dry.

2

Dice the cucumber, without peeling. Dice the beetroot (beets).

3

Halve and seed the grapes. Cut the rind and pith from the oranges. Cut the flesh into quarters lengthways and thinly slice the quarters, or simply peel the tangerines or satsumas and pull them into segments.

4

Mix together the tamari or shoyu sauce and rice wine or dry sherry.

5

Heat the oil in a wok or large frying pan over medium heat. Put in the cucumber, beetroot (beets) and raisins, and stir ½ minute. Add the rice, and stir 1 minute to heat through.

6

Mix in the fruit. Stir for 1 minute more, and take the pan from the heat. Either serve immediately or leave to get cold.

Note: Not suitable for freezing.

HOT RICE SALAD

China

Imperial (Metric)	American
8 ounces (225g) long-grain brown rice	1 cup long-grain brown rice
3 ounces (85g) mushrooms	½ cup mushrooms
8 ounces (225g) Chinese cabbage	¼ pound Chinese cabbage
6 spring onions	6 scallions
2 tablespoons Chinese pickled vegetables	2 tablespoons Chinese pickled vegetables
3 Soy Eggs (page 34)	3 Soy Eggs (page 34)
4 tablespoons groundnut oil	4 tablespoons peanut oil
2 tablespoons tamari or shoyu sauce	2 tablespoons tamari or shoyu sauce

1

Boil the rice as for Boiled Rice (page 118). Tip it on to a flat plate to dry and cool.

2

Thinly slice the mushrooms. Shred the cabbage. Cut the spring onions (scallions) into 1-inch (2.5 cm) lengths. Chop the pickled vegetables.

3

Finely chop the eggs.

4

Heat the oil in a wok or large frying pan over high heat. Put in the mushrooms, and stir-fry 1 minute. Put in the cabbage and onions, and stir-fry 1 minute more.

5

Add the pickles, stir, and then mix in the rice. Add the eggs and tamari sauce. Stir to heat through, and serve as soon as possible.

Note: Not suitable for freezing.

CRISP RICE (RICE PADDIES)

China

Imperial (Metric)	American
8 ounces (225g) short-grain brown rice	1 cup short-grain brown rice
2 teaspoons groundnut or sesame oil	2 teaspoons peanut or sesame oil

1

Cook the rice in boiling water until very soft, about 45 minutes. Drain, run cold water through it, and drain again. Let cool completely.

2

Heat the oven to 120F/50C/gas under ¼. Coat a heavy frying pan or skillet with the oil. Put in the rice, and spread it out in an even layer. Place the pan over low heat for 5 minutes, or until the bottom layer of rice is crisp and brown.

3

Turn the rice out on to a baking sheet. Cut it into 2-inch (5 cm) squares, and gently ease them apart.

4

Put the rice in the oven for 12 hours, checking it frequently after 8 hours. The squares are dry when they are crisp enough for pieces to be broken off.

CONGEE (SOFT RICE)

China

Imperial (Metric)	American
8 ounces (225g) short-grain brown rice	1 cup short-grain brown rice
2½ pints (1.42 litres) water	6 cups water

1

Put the rice in a colander, and wash it under cold, running water. Drain.

2

Put the rice in a large saucepan with the 4 pints (2.28 litres or 10 cups) water, and bring it to a boil.

3

Cover. Turn down to heat to simmer, and place a heat-proof mat under the pan.

4

Cook the rice for 1½ to 2 hours, stirring it with a wooden spoon every 15 to 20 minutes. It should have the consistency of thin porridge and a bland flavour.

Note: Serve Congee with a sprinkling of tamari or shoyu sauce or with Chinese pickled vegetables. To freeze, cool completely and pack into rigid plastic containers. Thaw at room temperature, and reheat in a saucepan.

SAVOURY CONGEE WITH EGGS

China

Imperial (Metric)	American
8 ounces (225g) short-grain brown rice	1 cup short-grain brown rice
2½ pints (1.42 litres) water	6 cups water
6 ounces (175g) water chestnuts, sliced	1½ cups water chestnuts, sliced
2 tablespoons Chinese pickled vegetables	2 tablespoons Chinese pickled vegetables
4 tablespoons tamari or shoyu sauce	4 tablespoons tamari or shoyu sauce
4 eggs	4 eggs
Hot Black Bean and Tomato Sauce (page 178), optional	Hot Black Bean and Tomato Sauce (page 178), optional

1

Put the rice in a colander, and wash it under cold, running water. Drain.
Put the rice in a large saucepan with the 4 pints (2.28 litres or 10 cups)
water, and bring it to a boil.

2

Cover. Turn down the heat to simmer, and place a heat-proof mat under
the pan. Cook the rice for 30 minutes.

3

Stir, and add the water chestnuts. Cook a further 30 minutes. Stir again,
and add the pickled vegetables and tamari or shoyu sauce.

4

Cook 30 minutes more, or until the congee is the consistency of thin
porridge.

5

Break each egg into a cup. Gently tip into the rice. Cook, covered, a
further 2 to 3 minutes for the eggs to set.

6

Divide the rice among four bowls, each with an egg. Serve the Hot Black
Bean and Tomato Sauce separately.

Note: Not suitable for freezing.

RICE IN COCONUT MILK

Indonesia

Imperial (Metric)	American
8 ounces (225g) long-grain brown rice	1 cup long-grain brown rice
1 pint (570ml) medium-thick coconut milk	2½ cups medium-thick coconut milk
Pinch of sea salt	Pinch of sea salt
Flavouring 1:	Flavoring 1:
1 curry leaf	1 curry leaf
1-inch (2.5 cm) lemon grass, bruised or 1 teaspoon grated rind of lemon or lime	1-inch lemon grass, bruised or 1 teaspoon grated rind of lemon or lime
Flavouring 2:	Flavoring 2:
1 bay leaf	1 bay leaf
4-inch (10 cm) cinnamon stick	4-inch cinnamon stick

1

Put the rice in a saucepan with the coconut milk and salt.

2

Add either flavouring 1 or 2.

3

Bring the rice to a boil. Cover, and cook gently 40 to 45 minutes or until all the coconut milk has been absorbed and the rice is tender.

4

Let the rice sit, covered, for 10 minutes before serving.

Note: Not suitable for freezing.

YELLOW RICE

Indonesia

Imperial (Metric)	American
2 tablespoons groundnut oil	2 tablespoons peanut oil
8 ounces (225g) long-grain brown rice	1 cup long-grain brown rice
1 pint (570ml) vegetable stock	2½ cups vegetable stock
1 teaspoon ground turmeric	1 teaspoon ground turmeric
4-inch (10cm) cinnamon stick	4-inch cinnamon stick
1 clove	1 clove
½ teaspoon ground cumin	½ teaspoon ground cumin
¼ teaspoon ground coriander	½ teaspoon ground coriander
1 bay leaf	1 bay leaf
2 fresh red chillies	2 fresh red chilis

1

Heat the oil in a saucepan over low heat. Put in the rice, and stir it for 2 minutes.

2

Add the turmeric, and stir 1 minute.

3

Pour in the stock, and bring it to a boil. Add the cinnamon, cloves, coriander and bay leaf.

4

Cover and simmer 40 to 45 minutes, or until the rice is tender and all the liquid has been absorbed. Let stand, covered, for 10 minutes.

5

Halve, core and seed the chillies. Cut them into thin strips.

6

Put the rice in a serving dish, and scatter the chillies over the top.

Note: Not suitable for freezing.

YELLOW RICE IN COCONUT MILK

Indonesia

Imperial (Metric)	American
8 ounces (225g) long-grain brown rice	1 cup long-grain brown rice
½ pint (285ml) water	1¼ cups water
Pinch of sea salt	Pinch of sea salt
½ pint (285ml) medium-thick coconut milk	1¼ cups medium-thick coconut milk
1 teaspoon ground turmeric	1 teaspoon ground turmeric
1 bay leaf	1 bay leaf
2 curry leaves, optional	2 curry leaves, optional
¼ teaspoon Laos powder, optional	¼ teaspoon Laos powder, optional
2 fresh, red chillies	2 fresh, red chilis

1

Put the rice in a saucepan with the water and salt. Bring to a boil. Cover, and cook gently for 20 minutes or until all the water has been absorbed.

2

Add the coconut milk, turmeric, bay leaf, curry leaves and Laos powder. Bring to a boil again.

3

Cover and cook very gently a further 20 to 25 minutes or until all the liquid has been absorbed and the rice is soft.

4

Serve garnished with the chillies as for yellow rice.

Note: Not suitable for freezing.

NASI GORENG

Indonesian Fried Rice

Imperial (Metric)	American
8 ounces (225g) long-grain brown rice	1 cup long-grain brown rice
4 shallots or 1 small onion	4 shallots or 1 small onion
2 fresh, red chillies	2 fresh, red chilis
4 tablespoons groundnut oil	4 tablespoons peanut oil
2 eggs, beaten	2 eggs, beaten
1 tablespoon tamari or shoyu sauce	1 tablespoon tamari or shoyu sauce
2 teaspoons tomato ketchup	2 teaspoons ketchup
¼ large cucumber, finely diced	¼ large cucumber, finely diced
8 ounces (225g) tomatoes	2 small tomatoes

1

Boil the rice as for Boiled Rice. Tip it on to a plate to cool and dry.

2

Finely chop the shallots or onion. Core, seed and chop the chillies.

3

Heat 2 tablespoons oil in a large frying pan over medium heat. Pour in the eggs, and cook until they set into a flat omelette. Turn out the omelette, and cut it into thin strips.

4

Heat the remaining oil in the pan over medium heat. Put in the shallots or onion and chilli, and stir-fry 1 minute. Add the sauce and ketchup, and mix well.

5

Put in the rice, and stir-fry 1½ minutes, or until reheated. Put the rice in a serving dish, and garnish with the strips of egg, cucumber and tomato rings.

Note: The tomato ketchup in this recipe is obviously not authentic, but it makes a good replacement for shrimp paste, which is often used. If possible, buy sugar-free ketchup from health shops.

Note: Not suitable for freezing.

NASI GORENG WITH ONIONS AND MUSHROOMS

Indonesia

Make the Nasi Goreng as before, omitting the eggs. Slice the cucumber instead of dicing it, and reserve it with the tomatoes. Make the following garnish.

Imperial (Metric)	American
2 medium onions	2 medium onions
4 ounces (115g) button mushrooms	½ cup button mushrooms
3 tablespoons groundnut oil	3 tablespoons peanut oil
2 teaspoons paprika	2 teaspoons paprika
2 tablespoons tamari or shoyu sauce	2 tablespoons tamari or shoyu sauce

1

Thinly slice the onions and mushrooms.

2

Heat the oil in a large frying pan over medium heat. Put in the onions, and stir-fry 3 minutes, or until they begin to brown.

3

Put in the mushrooms. Stir-fry for 2 minutes.

4

Stir in the paprika and tamari or shoyu sauce. Cook over low heat 1 minute.

5

Put the Nasi Goreng in a serving dish. Spoon the onion and mushroom mixture over the top. Put the cucumber and tomato slices around the edge.

Note: Not suitable for freezing.

VINEGAR RICE IN SEAWEED ROLLS

Japan

Imperial (Metric)	American
Savoury Rice with Vinegar Dressing (page 135)	Savoury Rice with Vinegar Dressing (page 135)
6 Chinese or Japanese dried mushrooms	6 Chinese or Japanese dried mushrooms
1 tablespoon groundnut oil	1 tablespoon peanut oil
2 eggs, beaten	2 eggs, beaten
Four 7 × 8 inch (18 × 20 cm) sheets nori	Four 7 × 8 inch sheets nori
2 ounces (55g) watercress, finely chopped	1 cup watercress, finely chopped

1

Soak the mushrooms in hot water for 30 minutes. Drain, and cut into thin strips.

2

Heat the oil in a frying pan over medium heat. Pour in the eggs. Cook them to make a flat omelette. Tip out the omelette, and cut it into thin strips.

3

Pass the sheets of nori over a gas flame or hold them briefly over a hot plate on one side only. This will intensify their colour.

4

Spread a quarter of the rice over each sheet of nori. Place strips of mushroom, egg and some chopped watercress down the centre.

5

Roll up the nori, and let rest 5 minutes. Cut it into rings, $\frac{3}{4}$ inch (2cm) thick.

Note: These rings are usually accompanied by a pickle such as red pickled ginger.

Note: Not suitable for freezing.

133

RED-COOKED FESTIVAL RICE

Japan

This is normally prepared with Japanese sweet rice, but short-grain brown rice makes a good substitute.

Imperial (Metric)	American
8 ounces (225g) aduki beans	1 cup aduki beans
8 ounces (225g) short-grain brown rice	1 cup short-grain brown rice
1 tablespoon sesame seeds	1 tablespoon sesame seeds
$\frac{1}{4}$ teaspoon sea salt	$\frac{1}{4}$ teaspoon sea salt

1

The day before serving, put the beans in a saucepan with 2 pints (1.14 litres or 5 cups) cold water. Bring to a boil, and boil 10 minutes. Cover, and simmer 40 minutes, or until the beans are tender but still intact.

2

Drain the beans, reserving the liquid. Put the beans in a bowl, and cover with cold water.

3

Wash the rice, and put it in the bean liquid. Cover, and put it in the refrigerator for 8 hours.

4

Drain the rice, and discard the soaking liquid.

5

Mix the rice with 4 ounces (115g or $\frac{1}{2}$ cup) of the beans. (The other beans were used only for flavouring. Use them in a separate dish if wished.)

6

Put the beans and rice in a steamer. Push holes through the rice with the handle of a wooden spoon to let the steam through.

7

Bring a large pan of water to a boil. Lower in the steamer. Cook the rice and beans 1 hour 15 minutes, or until the rice is soft.

8

While the rice is cooking, heat a heavy frying pan over medium heat. Put in the sesame seeds, and stir until they brown and begin to pop. Pour into a bowl, and mix in the salt. Serve the rice sprinkled with the sesame seeds.

Note: Festival rice may be served with savoury or with sweet dishes. Not suitable for freezing.

SAVOURY RICE WITH VINEGAR DRESSING

Japan

Imperial (Metric)	American
8 ounces (225g) long-grain brown rice	1 cup long-grain brown rice
1 pint (570ml) water	2½ cups water
2-inch square (5 cm) kombu	2-inch square kombu
Dressing:	Dressing:
3 tablespoons Japanese rice vinegar or white wine vinegar	3 tablespoons Japanese rice vinegar or white wine vinegar
1 tablespoon Barbados sugar	1 tablespoon brown sugar
2 tablespoons sake or dry sherry	2 tablespoons sake or dry sherry
¼ teaspoon sea salt	¼ teaspoon sea salt

1

Put the rice in a saucepan with the water and kombu. Bring it to a boil. Cover, and cook gently 40 to 45 minutes or until the rice is soft and all the liquid has been absorbed. Discard the kombu.

2

While the rice is cooking, make the dressing. Put all the ingredients in a saucepan, and bring them to a boil. Take the pan off the heat.

3

Transer the rice to a serving dish. Pour the hot dressing over it.

4

Cool to room temperature before serving.

Note: Not suitable for freezing.

The staple food of the north of China is wheat rather than rice, and from here come the delicious egg noodles which can be boiled and then stir-fried, simmered in stock, made into a salad or deep-fried. From other parts of China come the rice-stick noodles, which are made from rice flour and are flat, ribbon-like and white, and the transparent or cellophane noodles, which look like transparent vermicelli and are made from ground haricot (kidney) beans. Both rice-stick and transparent noodles should be soaked for a short time in warm water before being stir-fried or added to other dishes.

The other eastern country to use noodles is Japan. Japanese noodles are made from refined wheat flour. They are pure white and resemble either very thin spaghetti or long strips of very narrow tagliatelle. Thin noodles should be cooked for 6 to 7 minutes in boiling water and the wide noodles for 20 minutes.

EGG NOODLES IN YELLOW BEAN SAUCE

China

Imperial (Metric)	American
12 ounces (340g) egg noodles	¾ pound egg noodles
3 tablespoons yellow bean paste	3 tablespoons yellow bean paste
2 teaspoons chilli sauce	2 teaspoons chili sauce
1 garlic clove, crushed	1 garlic clove, crushed
2 green peppers	2 green peppers
1 medium onion	1 medium onion
3 tablespoons groundnut oil	3 tablespoons peanut oil
5 ounces (150g) bean sprouts	2¼ cups bean sprouts

1
Cook the noodles in boiling salted water for 5 minutes. Drain.

2
Mix together the yellow bean paste, chilli sauce and garlic.

3
Core and seed the peppers. Thinly slice the onion.

4
Heat the oil in a wok or large frying pan over high heat. Put in the peppers, onion and bean sprouts, and stir-fry 2 minutes.

5
Add the noodles, and stir in the sauce mixture. Heat through, and transfer to a warm serving dish.

Note: Not suitable for freezing.

NOODLES WITH BEAN PASTE SAUCE

China

Imperial (Metric)	American
12 ounces (340g) egg noodles	¾ pound egg noodles
8 ounces (225g) carrots	1½ cups carrots
½ large cucumber	½ large cucumber
6 spring onions	6 scallions
3 fl ounces (90ml) black bean paste	⅓ cup black bean paste
4 ounces (115g) Red Bean Paste, made with cooked red beans (page 172)	½ cup Red Bean Paste, made with cooked red beans (page 172)
4 tablespoons tamari or shoyu sauce	4 tablespoons tamari or shoyu sauce
1 tablespoon Chinese rice wine or dry sherry	1 tablespoon Chinese rice wine or dry sherry
2 tablespoons groundnut oil	2 tablespoons peanut oil
4 ounces (115g) bean sprouts	2 cups bean sprouts
1 garlic clove, crushed	1 garlic clove, crushed

1

Cook the noodles in lightly salted boiling water for 5 minutes. Drain, and keep warm.

2

Cut the carrots into matchstick pieces. Bring a pan of water to a boil. Put in the carrots, and cook for 2 minutes. Drain, and keep warm.

3

Cut the cucumber into matchstick pieces. Cut the spring onions (scallions) diagonally into 1-inch (2.5 cm) lengths.

4

Put the black bean sauce in a bowl, and gradually beat in first the red bean paste and then the rice wine or sherry and tamari or shoyu sauce. (Alternatively, work these ingredients together in a blender or food processor).

5

Heat the oil in a wok or large frying pan over high heat. Put in the spring onions (scallions), and stir-fry 1 minute. Put in the sauce, and stir to bring it to a boil.

6

Put the noodles in the pan, and stir to coat them in the sauce.

7

Put the noodles in a bowl, and toss in the carrots, cucumber, bean sprouts and garlic.

Note: Not suitable for freezing.

TOSSED NOODLES WITH RAW VEGETABLES

China

Imperial (Metric)	American
12 ounces (340g) egg noodles	¾ pound egg noodles
2 tablespoons sesame oil	2 tablespoons sesame oil
4 spring onions, chopped	4 scallions, chopped
Sauce:	Sauce:
1 tablespoon groundnut oil	1 tablespoon peanut oil
4 tablespoons tamari or shoyu sauce	4 tablespoons tamari or shoyu sauce
3 fl ounces (90ml) hoisin sauce	⅓ cup hoisin sauce
4 tablespoons Chinese rice wine or dry sherry	4 tablespoons Chinese rice wine or dry sherry
6 ounces (170g) bean sprouts	3 cups bean sprouts
½ large cucumber, diced	½ large cucumber, diced
4 ounces (115g) radish, cut into thin strips	⅔ cup radish, cut into thin strips
4 fl ounces (125ml) white wine vinegar	½ cup white wine vinegar

1

Cook the noodles in lightly salted boiling water for 5 minutes. Drain. Toss with the sesame oil. Divide among four small bowls, and keep warm.

2

Heat the oil in a wok or frying pan over high heat. Stir in the tamari or shoyu sauce, hoisin sauce and wine or sherry. Stir 1 minute, and remove the pan from the heat.

3

Scatter the spring onions (scallions) over the bowls of noodles. Either divide the sauce among four tiny bowls or put it into a central bowl on the table. Divide the vegetables among four plates or put them on one. Do the same with the vinegar. To serve, give each person a bowl of noodles. Let them help themselves to hot sauce and the contrasting crunchy vegetables, and toss them with the noodles.

Note: Not suitable for freezing.

FRIED NOODLES WITH MIXED VEGETABLES

China

Imperial (Metric)	American
12 ounces (340g) egg noodles	¾ pound egg noodles
4 ounces (114g) Chinese cabbage	¼ pound Chinese cabbage
2 green peppers	2 sweet green peppers
4 ounces (115g) mushrooms	½ cup mushrooms
1 medium onion	1 medium onion
4 tablespoons groundnut oil	4 tablespoons peanut oil
1 garlic clove, finely chopped	1 garlic clove, finely chopped
2 tablespoons tamari or shoyu sauce	2 tablespoons tamari or shoyu sauce

1

Cook the noodles in lightly salted water for 5 minutes. Drain.

2

Finely shred the cabbage. Core and seed the peppers, and cut into 1-inch (2.5 cm) strips. Thinly slice the mushrooms and onion.

3

Heat the oil in a wok or large frying pan over high heat. Put in the vegetables, and stir-fry 2 minutes.

4

Mix in the noodles, and stir-fry a further 2 minutes.

5

Add the tamari or shoyu sauce, and stir to heat through.

Note: Not suitable for freezing.

NOODLES IN SMOKING OIL

China

Imperial (Metric)	American
12 ounces (340g) egg noodles	¾ pound egg noodles
3 tablespoons tamari or shoyu sauce	3 tablespoons tamari or shoyu sauce
1 garlic clove, crushed	1 garlic clove, crushed
1 teaspoon grated, fresh ginger root	1 teaspoon grated fresh ginger
5 tablespoons groundnut oil	5 tablespoons peanut oil
4 spring onions, finely chopped	4 scallions, finely chopped

1

Cook the noodles in lightly salted boiling water. Drain. Put them in a wok or large frying pan.

2

Mix together the tamari or shoyu sauce, garlic and ginger. Fold the mixture into the noodles. Set the pan over high heat.

3

Heat the oil in a small frying pan until smoking. Pour it over the noodles, and stir until the noodles are very hot.

4

Mix in half the spring onions (scallions), and take the pan off the heat.

5

Put the noodles in a warm serving dish, and scatter the remaining spring onions (scallions) over the top.

Note: Not suitable for freezing.

NOODLE SALAD

China

Imperial (Metric)	American
8 ounces (225g) egg noodles	½ pound egg noodles
8 ounces (225g) carrots	2 to 3 small carrots
1 iceberg lettuce	1 iceberg lettuce
3 spring onions	3 scallions
2 tablespoons white wine vinegar	2 tablespoons white wine vinegar
2 tablespoons tamari or shoyu sauce	2 tablespoons tamari or shoyu sauce
1 teaspoon honey	1 teaspoon honey
1 tablespoon sesame oil	1 tablespoon sesame oil
1 tablespoon chopped, pickled ginger, or ½ teaspoon ground ginger mixed with 2 teaspoons lemon juice	1 tablespoon chopped, pickled ginger or ½ teaspoon ground ginger mixed with 2 teaspoons lemon juice

1

Cook the egg noodles in lightly salted boiling water for 5 minutes. Drain, and run cold water through them. Chill by plunging them into iced water and leaving them for 5 minutes. Drain again.

2

Cut the carrots into matchstick pieces. Bring a pan of water to a boil. Put in the carrots, and cook 2 minutes. Drain, and run cold water through them. Leave until completely cold.

3

Shred the lettuce. Cut the spring onions (scallions) diagonally into 1-inch (2.5 cm) pieces.

4

Mix together the vinegar, tamari or shoyu sauce, honey and sesame oil.

5

In a large bowl, toss the noodles with the carrots and lettuce. Mix in the pickled ginger or ground ginger and lemon juice. Fold in the dressing.

Note: Variation. Add 2 teaspoons tahini (sesame paste) to the dressing. Not suitable for freezing.

COLD-MIXED NOODLES WITH HOT SESAME SAUCE

China

Imperial (Metric)	American
12 ounces (340g) egg noodles	¾ pound egg noodles
2 tablespoons sesame oil	2 tablespoons sesame oil
Sauce:	Sauce:
2 tablespoons tahini (sesame paste)	2 tablespoons tahini (sesame paste)
3 fl ounces (90ml) tamari or shoyu sauce	⅓ cup tamari or shoyu sauce
4 tablespoons sesame oil	4 tablespoons sesame oil
1 tablespoon white wine vinegar	1 tablespoon white wine vinegar
1 teaspoon honey	1 teaspoon honey
1 teaspoon chilli sauce	1 teaspoon chili sauce
¼ teaspoon Szechuan Pepper and Salt Mixture (page 175)	¼ teaspoon Szechuan Pepper and Salt Mixture (page 175)
1 spring onion, finely chopped	1 scallion, finely chopped
½ ounce (15g) fresh ginger root, peeled and grated	½ ounce fresh ginger, peeled and grated
1 garlic clove, crushed	1 garlic clove, crushed
Garnish:	Garnish:
½ large cucumber	½ large cucumber
12 radishes	12 radishes
4 ounces (115g) bean sprouts	2 cups bean sprouts

1

Cook the noodles in lightly salted, boiling water for 5 minutes. Drain, and run cold water through them. Chill by putting them in ice water and leaving them for 5 minutes. Drain again. Toss with the sesame oil.

2

To make the sauce, put the sesame paste in a bowl, and gradually beat in the tamari or shoyu sauce, and then the oil and vinegar. Mix in the remaining sauce ingredients. Cut the cucumber into matchstick pieces. Thinly slice the radishes, and cut them into small shreds. To serve, divide the noodles among four bowls and the sauce between four tiny bowls. On each of four small plates put a portion of cucumber, radishes and beansprouts. The idea is to let each person mix his or her own noodles according to taste.

Note: Not suitable for freezing.

TRANSPARENT NOODLES WITH BLACK BEAN SAUCE

China

Imperial (Metric)	American
5 ounces (140g) transparent noodles	5 oz transparent noodles
4 spring onions	4 scallions
1 green chilli	1 green chili
1 tablespoon black bean paste	1 tablespoon black bean paste
3 fl ounces (90ml) vegetable stock	⅓ cup vegetable stock
2 tablespoons tamari or shoyu sauce	2 tablespoons tamari or shoyu sauce
4 tablespoons groundnut oil	4 tablespoons peanut oil

1

Soak the noodles in warm water for 10 minutes. Drain.

2

Finely chop the spring onions (scallions). Core, seed and finely chop the chilli.

3

Mix together the black bean paste, vegetable stock and tamari or shoyu sauce.

4

Heat the oil in a wok or large frying pan over high heat. Stir in the onions and chilli, and stir-fry 1 minute.

5

Pour in the bean paste mixture, and put in the noodles. Bring to a boil, and stir 1 minute, or until most of the liquid has evaporated.

Note: To freeze, cool completely and pack into containers. Cover and store for up to one month in the freezer. Thaw at room temperature, and reheat in a frying pan or wok over medium heat.

Note: Not suitable for freezing.

CRISPY NOODLES WITH MIXED VEGETABLES

China

Imperial (Metric)	American
8 Chinese mushrooms	8 Chinese mushrooms
8 ounces (225g) Chinese cabbage	½ pound Chinese cabbage
One 8 oz (225g) tin bamboo shoots	1 cup bamboo shoots
Half an 8 oz (225g) tin water chestnuts	½ cup water chestnuts
1 medium onion	1 medium onion
2 teaspoons arrowroot	2 teaspoons arrowroot
2 tablespoons tamari or shoyu sauce	2 tablespoons tamari or shoyu sauce
8 ounces (225g) egg noodles	½ pound egg noodles
4 tablespoons groundnut oil	4 tablespoons peanut oil
Oil for deep frying	Oil for deep frying

1

Soak the Chinese mushrooms in boiling water for 30 minutes. Drain, reserving the water. Cut into quarters.

2

Shred the cabbage. Thinly slice the bamboo shoots and water chestnuts.

3

Mix the arrowroot with the tamari or shoyu sauce and 4 tablespoons of the mushroom water.

4

Cook the noodles in lightly salted boiling water for 5 minutes. Drain, and divide them into four portions.

5

Heat the 4 tablespoons oil in a wok or large frying pan over high heat. Put in the onion, and stir-fry 1 minute. Add the Chinese cabbage, bamboo shoots, water chestnuts and mushrooms, and stir-fry a further 2 minutes. Pour in the arrowroot mixture, and stir until it boils and thickens.

6

Remove the pan from the heat, and keep the vegetables warm.

7

Heat a pan of deep oil to 350F/180C. Put in one portion of the noodles, keeping them together in an even, round shape. Deep-fry about 6 minutes, or until crisp and brown, turning once. Lift out the noodles, and drain on paper towels.

8

Reheat the oil, and cook the remaining portions of noodles in the same way.

9

To serve, divide the vegetables among four plates or bowls, and top each with a portion of crispy noodles.

Note: The noodles are not suitable for freezing. The vegetable mixture may be cooled and frozen in plastic containers. Thaw at room temperature, and reheat in a saucepan.

HOT, MARINATED AUBERGINES (EGGPLANT) WITH TRANSPARENT NOODLES

China

Imperial (Metric)	American
1 pint (570ml) Hot Marinating Sauce (page 174)	2½ cups Hot Marinating Sauce (page 174)
1 lb (455g) aubergine	1 pound eggplant
1 tablespoon sea salt	1 tablespoon sea salt
¼ large cucumber	¼ large cucumber
4 ounces (115g) transparent noodles	4 ounces transparent noodles
Oil for deep-frying	Oil for deep-frying
4 tablespoons groundnut oil	4 tablespoons peanut oil
2 tablespoons tamari or shoyu sauce	2 tablespoons tamari or shoyu sauce
4 fl ounces (125ml) vegetable stock	½ cup vegetable stock
2 tablespoons fresh coriander	2 tablespoons fresh cilantro

1

Cut the aubergine (eggplant) into ½-inch (1.5cm) slices. Put them into a colander, and sprinkle with the sea salt. Leave for 20 minutes to drain. Run cold water through them to wash them, and dry them with paper towels.

2

Cut the cucumber into matchstick pieces.

3

Soak the noodles in warm water for 15 minutes. Drain.

4

Bring the Hot Marinating Sauce to a boil in a saucepan. Put in the aubergine (eggplant) slices, and simmer very gently for 10 minutes. Drain.

5

Heat a pan of deep oil to 350F/180C. Put in the aubergine (eggplant) slices, about 5 at a time, and cook 3 minutes, or until crisp on the outside but still soft in the middle. Lift out, and drain on paper towels.

6

Heat the oil in a wok or large frying pan over medium heat. Put in the cucumber, and stir-fry 1 minute.

7

Add the noodles, and lower the heat. Stir for 2 minutes.

8

Add the tamari or shoyu sauce and vegetable stock. Cook over medium heat 2 minutes.

9

Add the aubergine (eggplant) slices, and turn in the other ingredients to heat through.

10

Put the aubergines (eggplant) and noodles in a warm serving dish, and scatter the fresh coriander (cilantro) over the top.

Note: Not suitable for freezing.

CELLOPHANE NOODLES AND STEAMED EGG

China

Imperial (Metric)	American
1 ounce (30g) transparent noodles	1 ounce transparent noodles
6 eggs	6 eggs
4 spring onions finely chopped	4 scallions, finely chopped
2 tablespoons Chinese rice wine or dry sherry	2 tablespoons Chinese rice wine or dry sherry
4 tablespoons tamari or shoyu sauce	4 tablespoons tamari or shoyu sauce
1 teaspoon sesame oil	1 teaspoon sesame oil

1

Break the noodles into 1½-inch (4 cm) lengths. Soak in warm water for 30 minutes. Drain.

2

Beat the eggs. Mix in the onions, wine or sherry and half the tamari or shoyu sauce. Mix in the noodles.

3

Pour the mixture into a heat-proof dish, and cover with foil. Place the dish in a steamer.

4

Lower the steamer into a large pan of boiling water, and steam the egg mixture for 30 minutes, or until set.

5

Take the dish from the steamer. Mix together the remaining tamari or shoyu sauce and the sesame oil. Sprinkle them over the top of the egg. Serve straight from the dish.

Note: Not suitable for freezing.

TOSS-FRIED RICE NOODLES

China

Imperial (Metric)	American
12 ounces (340g) rice-stick noodles	¾ pound rice-stick noodles
8 ounces (225g) leeks	2 medium leeks
4 large celery sticks	4 large celery stalks
4 ounces (115g) drained, tinned bamboo shoots	½ cup drained, canned bamboo shoots
1 small onion	1 small onion
4 tablespoons groundnut oil	4 tablespoons peanut oil
1 garlic clove, finely chopped	1 garlic clove, finely chopped
2 tablespoons tamari or shoyu sauce	2 tablespoons tamari or shoyu sauce
2 tablespoons vegetable stock	2 tablespoons vegetable stock

1

Soak the noodles in warm water for 15 minutes to soften. Drain.

2

Cut the leeks and celery into matchstick pieces. Thinly slice the bamboo shoots and onion.

3

Heat half the oil in a wok or frying pan over high heat. Put in the leeks, celery, bamboo shoots, onion and garlic and stir-fry 2 minutes. Remove.

4

Add the remaining oil, and put in the noodles. Stir-fry for 2 minutes.

5

Add the vegetables, and fold in so as not to break up the noodles.

6

Add the tamari sauce and stock, and stir 2 minutes or until the liquid has evaporated.

Note: To freeze, cool completely, pack into rigid containers and cover. Store for up to one month. Thaw at room temperature, and reheat in a saucepan.

Note: Not suitable for freezing.

151

HOT NOODLES IN BROTH WITH EGG

Japan

Imperial (Metric)	American
10 ounces (285g) wide Japanese noodles	10 ounces wide Japanese noodles
1 teaspoon sea salt	1 teaspoon sea salt
1¾ pints (1 litre) kombu stock	4 cups kombu stock
2 tablespoons tamari or shoyu sauce	2 tablespoons tamari or shoyu sauce
4 small eggs	4 small eggs
4-inch (10 cm) square nori	4-inch square nori
2 spring onions, finely chopped	2 scallions, finely chopped

1

Bring a large pan of water to a boil. Put in the noodles, and bring them back to a boil. Cook, uncovered, over a moderate heat for 20 minutes, or until very soft. Add the salt, and take the pan from the heat. Leave the noodles in the water, covered, for 5 minutes. Drain, and run cold water through them for 5 minutes. Drain again.

2

Bring the stock to a boil in a saucepan. Add the tamari or shoyu sauce. Put in the noodles. Bring back to a boil, and boil for 1 minute to heat through.

3

Pour the noodles and broth into four large soup bowls.

4

While the noodles are still hot, break an egg into each bowl.

5

Sprinkle the nori and spring onions (scallions) over the top.

6

Serve as soon as the heat from the soup has lightly cooked the eggs.

Note: The noodles in broth can be frozen. Thaw at room temperature and reheat in a saucepan. Do not freeze after the eggs have been added.

COLD SUMMER NOODLES

Japan

Imperial (Metric)	American
10 ounces (285g) thin, Japanese noodles	10 ounces thin, Japanese noodles
12 ice cubes	12 ice cubes
½ ounce (15g) fresh ginger root, peeled and grated	½ ounce fresh ginger, peeled and grated
4 spring onions, finely chopped	4 scallions, finely chopped
Sauce:	Sauce:
3 tablespoons sake or dry sherry	3 tablespoons sake or dry sherry
3 fl ounces (90ml) tamari or shoyu sauce	⅓ cup tamari or shoyu sauce
4 fl ounces (125ml) kombu stock	½ cup kombu stock
5 teaspoons flaked, dried bonito	5 teaspoons flaked, dried bonito

1

Make the sauce. Heat the sake or sherry in a saucepan over moderate heat until lukewarm. Ignite it, and shake the pan gently until the flame dies. Add half the tamari or shoyu sauce, the kombu stock and dried bonito. Bring to a boil, and strain through a sieve. Cool completely, and add the remaining tamari or shoyu sauce.

2

Bring a large pan of water to a boil. Put in the noodles, and bring back to a boil, stirring occasionally. Cook, uncovered, over moderate heat for 6 to 7 minutes, or until very soft. Drain, run cold water through them for 5 minutes, and drain again.

3

Divide the noodles among four bowls. Put three ice cubes into each bowl.

4

Divide the sauce among four tiny bowls. On each of four very small plates put ½ teaspoon grated ginger root and 1 finely chopped spring onion (scallion).

5

Each person can then mix and flavour his own noodles according to taste.

Note: Not suitable for freezing.

FOX NOODLES

Japan

According to Japanese legend the fox's favourite food is fried bean curd. These noodles topped with bean curd are therefore called Fox Noodles.

Imperial (Metric)	American
6 ounces (170g) bean curd	6 ounces bean curd
Oil for deep frying	Oil for deep-frying
10 ounces (285g) wide, Japanese noodles	10 oz wide, Japanese noodles
1 teaspoon sea salt	1 teaspoon sea salt
2 pints (1.14 litres) kombu stock	5 cups kombu stock
4 tablespoons tamari or shoyu sauce	4 tablespoons tamari or shoyu sauce
4-inch (10 cm) square nori, crumbled	4-inch square nori, crumbled
2 spring onions, finely chopped	2 scallions, finely chopped

1

Cut the bean curd into ¼-inch (6 mm) thick slices. Lay them on a plate, and cover with foil. Place a heavy saucepan on top, and leave for 30 minutes. Drain off all the liquid that has collected.

2

Bring a large pan of water to a boil. Put in the noodles, and bring back to a boil. Cook, uncovered, over moderate heat for 20 minutes, or until very soft. Add the salt, and take the pan from the heat. Leave the noodles in the water, covered, for 5 minutes. Drain, run cold water through them for 5 minutes. Drain again.

3

Put ¼ pint (140 ml or ⅔ cup) of the stock in a saucepan with half the tamari or shoyu sauce and the nori. Bring to a boil, and simmer 2 minutes. Strain the mixture through a sieve.

4

Heat a 1½-inch (4 cm) depth of oil in a frying pan to a temperature of 350F/180C. Put in the pieces of bean curd about 4 at a time. Deep-fry until golden. Remove from the heat. Drain on paper towels.

5

Put the nori-flavoured stock in a small saucepan. Set it over high heat, and bring it to a boil. Put in the bean curd. Boil for about 5 minutes, or until the liquid has been reduced to about 4 tablespoons. Take the pan from the heat.

6

Put the remaining stock and tamari or shoyu sauce in a large saucepan. Bring to a boil. put in the noodles, and bring back to a boil. Take the pan from the heat.

7

Pour the noodles with their broth into four large soup bowls. Top with the bean curd and a sprinkling of spring onions (scallions).

Note: The noodles in broth can be frozen in rigid containers and stored for up to one month. The bean curd is not suitable for freezing.

Chapter 8
Pancakes, Breads and Dim Sum Dishes

Wheat is a scarce crop in the East, except in the north of China. From here come steamed breads and the flat pancakes that are served with spicy and heavily sauced dishes.

From the Canton area of China comes the Dim Sum meal. Translated, it means 'to please the heart,' and the meal should be an agreeable snack, enjoyed at a local restaurant with friends in the middle of the afternoon or morning. The main feature of a Dim Sum meal is the selection of steamed buns which are filled with either savoury or sweet fillings.

Crispy pancake rolls and egg rolls have become popular as Chinese snacks in the West. They are best eaten alone as a light meal rather than in a mixture of other dishes as they can so often be when eaten in a Chinese restaurant.

The deep-fried pancakes from Japan also make a perfect light meal.

156

MANDARIN PANCAKES

China

Imperial (Metric)	American
1 pound (455g) wholewheat flour	4 cups whole wheat flour
½ pint (285ml) boiling water	1¼ cups boiling water
1 tablespoon groundnut oil	1 tablespoon peanut oil
3 tablespoons sesame oil	3 tablespoons sesame oil

1

Put the flour into a mixing bowl, and make a well in the centre. Mix together the water and oil, and gradually stir them into the flour, using chopsticks or a wooden spoon. Turn the dough on to a floured worktop, and knead it until it is firm. Let rest 10 minutes.

2

Divide the dough into three portions, and roll each piece into a sausage shape about 2 inches (5 cm) in diameter. Cut each roll into eight. Roll the small pieces into thin pancakes of about 7 inches (18 cm) in diameter.

3

Brush one side of half the pancakes with the sesame oil. Sandwich them together with the remaining pancakes.

4

Set a heavy frying pan over high heat without fat. When the pan is hot, reduce the heat to moderate. Fry one pancake at a time, turning it over when it starts to rise and bubble and when small brown spots appear on the underside. When both sides are done, remove the pancake to a plate.

5

Gently peel the two pancakes apart, and fold each one in half, oiled side inwards.

6

Prepare the remaining pancakes in the same way, keeping them warm in a low oven as the rest are cooked.

Note: These pancakes can be made in advance, wrapped in a clean linen tea towel and reheated in a low oven when needed. Not suitable for freezing.

MUSHROOM AND SPRING ONION (SCALLION) PACKAKES

China

Imperial (Metric)	American
Half quantity pancake dough as for Mandarin Pancakes	Half quantity pancake dough as for Mandarin Pancakes
4 ounces (115g) mushrooms	½ cup mushrooms
2 tablespoons groundnut oil	2 tablespoons peanut oil
2 tablespoons rice wine or dry sherry	2 tablespoons rice wine or dry sherry
Pinch of sea salt	Pinch of sea salt
6 spring onions	6 scallions
Oil for shallow frying	Oil for shallow frying

1
Finely chop the mushrooms.

2
Heat the 2 tablespoons oil in a frying pan over high heat. Put in the mushrooms, and stir-fry 1 minute. Add the wine or sherry, and stir-fry 30 seconds. Add the salt, and take the pan from the heat. Put the mushrooms in a bowl. Finely chop the spring onions (scallions). Mix into the mushrooms.

3
Divide the pancake dough into two, and roll each piece into a sausage shape about 2 inches (5 cm) in diameter. Cut each piece into six.

4
Roll each small piece of dough into a thin, flat, oval shape.

5
Scatter about 1 tablespoon of the mushroom and spring onion (scallion) filling over each one.

6
Fold in two long sides of each pancake to the centre. Fold the pancake in half lengthways. Form it into a round, flat coil, and tuck in the end. Roll the coil flat.

Note: Not suitable for freezing.

8

Shallow-fry each pancake in 2 tablespoons oil over moderate heat until brown on both sides.

Note: These should be served hot, with savoury dishes.

DOUGH FOR STEAMED ROLLS AND BUNS

China

Imperial (Metric)	American
1 ounce (25g) fresh yeast or ½ ounce (15g) dried	2 tablespoons fresh yeast or 1 tablespoon dried
2 teaspoons Barbados sugar	2 teaspoons brown sugar
3 tablespoons warm water	3 tablespoons warm water
1 pound (455g) wholewheat flour	4 cups whole wheat flour
½ pint (285ml) milk, warmed	1¼ cups milk, warmed

1

If you are using fresh yeast, crumble it into a bowl, add the sugar, and pour in the water. If you are using dried, dissolve the sugar in the water and sprinkle the yeast on top. Leave the yeast in a warm place until it begins to froth.

2

Put the flour in a mixing bowl. Make a well in the centre. Pour in the yeast mixture and the milk. Mix everything to a dough.

3

Turn the dough on to a floured work surface, and knead until smooth. Return to the bowl. Cover with a clean cloth, or put it into a greased polythene (plastic) bag. Leave in a warm place for 1 hour to double in size.

4

Punch down the dough with your fist. Cover it again, and let sit for 30 minutes, or until it has doubled in size again.

5

Knead the dough until smooth and elastic.

Note: Not suitable for freezing.

MAKING FLOWER ROLLS

China

Flower rolls are plain bread rolls in the shape of a flower, made from steamed bread dough (see previous page for recipe). They should be served hot, with savoury dishes.

1

Divide the dough in two. Roll each piece into a rectangle about 8 by 12 inches (20 by 30 cm).

2

Lightly brush the dough with sesame oil. A little chopped raw onion can be scattered over the surface if wished.

3

Roll up the dough from one long side into a cylinder about 1½ inches (4 cm) in diameter. Cut the roll into ¾-inch (2 cm) lengths.

4

Push the lengths together firmly in two's, rounded sides together.

5

Hold the outside edge of each of the joined pieces with your thumb and forefinger. Gently pull backwards until they meet in the centre along the first join. The oiled layers of the dough should separate like a flower. Seal these pulled edges together.

6

Find two or more heat-proof plates each about ½ inch (1.5 cm) less in diameter than the steamer you are going to use. Place the shaped rolls on these plates no less than 1½ inches (4 cm) apart all round. Cover the rolls with clean dry tea towels, and leave in a warm place for 30 minutes to rise.

7

Bring a pan of water to a boil. Put one plate of the bread rolls into a steamer. Cover, and steam for 15 minutes, or until the dough is firm. Lift the plate out. Cook the remaining rolls in the same way. After the last batch has been steamed, put the others back for 3 to 4 minutes to heat through. Serve hot.

Note: Not suitable for freezing.

MAKING FILLED BUNS

China

A half quantity of the steamed bread dough (see page 159 for recipe) will make 12 filled buns.

1

Form the dough into a sausage shape, and cut it into 12 pieces.

2

Roll each piece into a 4-inch (10 cm) round. Put about 2 tablespoons of the filling in the centre of each one.

3

Loosely gather up the sides of the dough so that they meet at the top. Twist them round to secure the edges.

4

Put the buns on a sheet of floured, greaseproof (parchment or waxed) paper. Cover with a clean tea cloth, and leave for 30 minutes to rise.

5

Put the buns in a steamer, leaving a gap of at least 1 inch (2.5 cm) all round. Bring a pan of water to a boil. Lower in the steamer. Cover, and cook the buns for 10 minutes. If the buns have to be cooked in two batches, lift out the first and put in the second. Put those that were cooked first back into the steamer on top of those still cooking for the final 2 minutes of cooking time.

Note: Not suitable for freezing.

SPINACH AND LEEK STEAMED BUN STUFFING

China
(For 12 buns)

Imperial (Metric)	American
8 ounces (225g) spinach	2 cups spinach
4 ounces (115g) leeks	2 medium leeks
4 spring onions	4 scallions
3 tablespoons oil	¼ cup oil
1 tablespoon tamari or shoyu sauce	1 tablespoon tamari or shoyu sauce
1 tablespoon rice wine or dry sherry	1 tablespoon rice wine or dry sherry

1

Wash and drain the spinach. Shred fine. Thinly slice the leeks. Finely chop the spring onions (scallions).

2

Heat the oil in a wok or large frying pan over high heat. Put in the spinach, leeks and spring onions (scallions). Stir-fry for 3 minutes, or until beginning to wilt.

3

Add the sauce and wine or sherry. Bring to a boil. Mix well, and take the pan from the heat.

Note: Not suitable for freezing.

CHINESE CABBAGE AND BLACK BEAN STEAMED BUN STUFFING

China

For 12 buns

Imperial (Metric)	American
4 ounces (115g) Chinese cabbage	4 ounce Chinese cabbage
Half a 6 ounce (170g) tin black beans in salted sauce	Half a 6 ounce can black beans in salted sauce
2 spring onions, finely chopped	2 scallions, finely chopped

1

Finely chop the cabbage. Mix all the ingredients together and leave for 30 minutes in a cool place.

Note: Not suitable for freezing.

SWEET SESAME STEAMED BUN STUFFING

China

(For 12 buns)

Imperial (Metric)	American
4 ounces (115g) sesame seeds	$\frac{3}{4}$ cup sesame seeds
2 ounces (55g) Barbados sugar	$\frac{1}{2}$ cup brown sugar
3 tablespoons water	3 tablespoons water
3 tablespoons sesame oil	3 tablespoons sesame oil

1

Put all the ingredients in a saucepan. Set over low heat, and stir about 8 minutes, or until the mixture is smooth.

2

If wished, after the buns have been shaped each one may be dotted with a small amount of red food colouring.

DATE AND NUT STEAMED BUN STUFFING

China
(for 12 buns)

Imperial (Metric)	American
2 ounces (55g) Chinese red dates	2 ounces Chinese red dates
1 ounce (30g) shelled walnuts	2 tablespoons shelled walnuts
1 ounce (30g) shelled almonds	2 tablespoons shelled almonds
2 tablespoons Red Bean Paste (page 172)	2 tablespoons Red Bean Paste (page 172)
2 teaspoons sesame oil	2 teaspoons sesame oil

1

Stone (pit) the dates, and finely chop them.

2

Finely chop the walnuts and almonds.

3

Mix all the ingredients together.

Note: Not suitable for freezing.

WONTONS

China

Imperial (Metric)	American
1 pound (455g) wholewheat flour plus extra for rolling	4 cups whole wheat flour plus extra for rolling
1 teaspoon sea salt	1 teaspoon sea salt
2 eggs, beaten	2 eggs, beaten
7 fl ounces (200 ml) cold water	¾ cup cold water
Filling	Filling
Oil for deep frying	Oil for deep frying

1

Put the flour in a bowl. Make a well in the centre, and pour in the eggs and water. Mix the ingredients with your fingers until you can make a soft ball. Knead the dough in the bowl until smooth.

2

Divide the dough into four. Roll each piece to a thickness of $\frac{1}{16}$ inch (2 mm). Cut into 6 squares.

3

Place 1 teaspoon of filling in the centre of each wonton wrapper. Moisten the edges of the wrapper with water. Bring one corner of the wrapper over the filling to just on one side of the opposite corner. Bring the other corners together under the folded edge. Moisten with water, and pinch together. As each wonton is finished, place in a plastic bag to keep it moist.

4

To cook, heat a pan of deep oil to 375F/190C. Drop in the wontons about six at a time. Deep-fry for 2 minutes, or until crisp and golden. Drain on paper towels.

Note: Not suitable for freezing.

# BEAN CURD AND WATER CHESTNUT WONTONS

China

Imperial (Metric)	American
4 ounces (115g) bean curd	$\frac{1}{4}$ pound bean curd
2 tablespoons mashed, fermented bean curd	2 tablespoons mashed, fermented bean curd
4 water chestnuts, finely chopped	4 water chestnuts, finely chopped
2 spring onions, finely chopped	2 scallions, finely chopped

1

Finely chop the bean curd.

2

Mix it with the remaining ingredients.

Note: Not suitable for freezing.

SPRING ROLLS

China

(To make 8)

Imperial (Metric)	American
4 ounces (115g) wholewheat flour	1 cup whole wheat flour
½ pint (285ml) water	1⅓ cups water
Pinch of sea salt	Pinch of sea salt
Oil for greasing	Oil for greasing
Filling	Filling
Oil for deep frying	Oil for deep frying

1

Put the flour in a bowl. Beat in the water to make a batter. Beat in the salt. Let the batter stand for 30 minutes.

2

Lightly grease an 8-inch (20 cm) frying pan, and set it over high heat. Spoon in 3 tablespoons of the batter, and spread it out quickly. Cook on one side only until the batter has set to form a pancake. Remove it, and keep it warm. Cook the remaining batter in the same way.

3

Lay each pancake cooked side up. Put 2 tablespoons of the prepared filling on the bottom half of each pancake. Fold in the bottom edge. Fold in the sides. Roll up the pancake to make a tight roll.

4

Make a paste mixture by mixing 1 tablespoon each flour and water. Use this to seal the edges.

5

To cook, heat a pan of deep oil to 350F/180C. Deep-fry the rolls, two at a time, for about 3 minutes, or until golden brown.

Note: Not suitable for freezing.

VEGETABLE FILLING FOR SPRING ROLLS

China

(For 8 rolls)

Imperial (Metric)	American
1 green pepper	1 sweet green pepper
4 ounces (115g) mushrooms	½ cup mushrooms
2 celery sticks	2 celery stalks
3 tablespoons groundnut oil	3 tablespoons peanut oil
1 garlic clove, finely chopped	1 garlic clove, finely chopped
4 ounces (115g) bean sprouts	2 cups bean sprouts
3 tablespoons tamari or shoyu sauce	3 tablespoons tamari or shoyu sauce
2 tablespoons Chinese rice wine or dry sherry	2 tablespoons Chinese rice wine or dry sherry
1 tablespoon arrowroot	1 tablespoon arrowroot

1

Core, seed and finely chop the peppers. Thinly slice the mushrooms. Finely chop the celery.

2

Mix together the tamari or shoyu sauce, wine or sherry and arrowroot.

3

Heat the oil in a wok or large frying pan over high heat. Put in the pepper, mushrooms, celery, garlic and bean sprouts. Stir-fry 1 minute.

4

Pour in the arrowroot mixture, and stir until it thickens.

5

Take the pan from the heat. Cool the filling completely before finishing the pancakes.

Note: Not suitable for freezing.

EGG ROLLS

China

(To make 8)

Imperial (Metric)	American
3 ounces (85g) wholewheat flour	¾ cup whole wheat flour
½ pint (285ml) water	1⅓ cups water
6 eggs, beaten	6 eggs, beaten
Groundnut oil for greasing	Peanut oil for greasing
Filling	Filling
Oil for deep frying	Oil for deep frying

1

Put the flour in a bowl. Make a well in the centre. Gradually beat in first the water and then the eggs to make a smooth, thin batter.

2

Lightly grease a 7-inch (18 cm) frying pan. Pour in 3 tablespoons of the batter, and spread it out quickly. Cook the pancake on one side only, and remove it. Cook the remaining batter in the same way.

3

Place the pancakes cooked side up. Put 2 tablespoons of the filling on the bottom of each pancake. Fold over the bottom edge. Fold over the sides. Roll up the pancake. Dampen the edge with cold water to seal it.

4

To cook, heat a pan of deep oil to 350F/180C. Deep-fry the rolls, two at a time, for 10 minutes, or until golden brown. Drain on paper towels. Keep the finished pancakes warm in a low oven while you cook the rest.

Note: Not suitable for freezing.

CHINESE MUSHROOM FILLING FOR EGG ROLLS

China

(For 8 rolls)

Imperial (Metric)	American
8 Chinese mushrooms	8 Chinese mushrooms
3 ounces (85g) drained, tinned bamboo shoots	½ cup drained, canned bamboo shoots
3 ounces (85g) drained, tinned water chestnuts	½ cup drained, canned water chestnuts
4 spring onions	4 scallions
3 tablespoons groundnut oil	3 tablespoons peanut oil
8 ounces (225g) bean sprouts	4 cups bean sprouts
2 tablespoons tamari or shoyu sauce	2 tablespoons tamari or shoyu sauce
2 tablespoons Chinese rice wine or dry sherry	2 tablespoons Chinese rice wine or dry sherry
1 tablespoon arrowroot	1 tablespoon arrowroot

1

Soak the Chinese mushrooms in warm water for 30 minutes. Drain, and finely chop.

2

Thinly slice the bamboo shoots and water chestnuts.

3

Finely chop the spring onions (scallions).

4

Heat the oil in a wok or large frying pan over high heat. Put in the mushrooms, and stir-fry 1 minute. Put in the bamboo shoots, water chestnuts, spring onions (scallions) and bean sprouts. Stir-fry 2 minutes.

5

Mix together the tamari or shoyu sauce, wine or sherry and arrowroot. Stir them into the pan. Stir until the liquid boils and thickens.

6

Remove the pan from the heat, and cool the filling to room temperature.

Note: Not suitable for freezing.

DEEP-FRIED PANCAKES

Japan

Imperial (Metric)	American
1 medium carrot	1 medium carrot
½ ounce (15g) fresh ginger root	½ ounce fresh ginger
6 ounces (170g) shelled peas, fresh or frozen	1 cup shelled peas, fresh or frozen
8 fl ounces (225ml) tempura batter (page 103)	1 cup tempura batter (page 103)
1 ounce (30g) wholewheat flour	¼ cup whole wheat flour
Oil for deep frying	Oil for deep frying
Dipping sauce as for Tempura (page 103)	Dipping sauce as for Tempura (page 103)

1

Grate the carrot. Peel and grate the ginger root. Mix them in a bowl with the peas.

2

Mix in the batter. Sprinkle the flour over the top, and stir until well mixed in.

3

Bring a pan of deep oil to 375F/190C.

4

Put about 1½ tablespoons of the pancake mixture on a wide, flat metal slice. Flatten it down to a pancake of about 1½-inches (6.5 cm) round.

5

Slide the pancake into the oil. Make two more in the same way to cook with it. Cook them about 1 minute on each side, or until golden brown. Lift out, and drain on paper towels.

Note: These pancakes are served with the dipping sauce as a light lunch or as part of a Japanese meal. For a complete meal they are often placed on top of bowls of rice and the dipping sauce is poured over them. Not suitable for freezing.

Chapter 9
Bean Pastes, Sauces and Sambals

Bean pastes feature as flavourings in Chinese and Southeast Asian dishes. The yellow and black bean pastes are always used for savoury ingredients. The red bean paste is mostly used in sweet dishes, but it is occasionally used with one of the other pastes in a sauce.

Sweet and sour sauce is the best known of all the Chinese sauces, and, yes, it is possible to omit the sugar. For a change, try one of the other Chinese sauces. Simply spoon them over rice, as they are substantial enough or serve them with vegetables, egg dishes and bean curd.

In Southeast Asia the *sambal* is a frequent accompaniment to all savoury dishes. Roughly translated, *sambal* means relish. Small amounts are served to add flavour and zest to the meal, in much the same way we would use a mustard or a chutney.

RED BEAN PASTE

China

Imperial (Metric)	American
8 ounces (225g) kidney beans, soaked and cooked	1¼ cups kidney beans, soaked and cooked
2 ounces (55g) honey	1½ tablespoons honey

1

Rub the kidney beans through a vegetable mill or a wire sieve.

2

Beat in the honey.

Note: This is usually used for sweet dishes but is occasionally mixed with savoury ingredients to make sauces, for example, Noodles with Bean Paste Sauce (page 138).

Note: Not suitable for freezing.

BLACK BEAN PASTE

China

Imperial (Metric)	American
One 6-ounce (170g) tin black beans in salted sauce	One 6-ounce can black beans in salted sauce
2 tablespoons tamari or shoyu sauce	2 tablespoons tamari or shoyu sauce
2 teaspoons chilli sauce	2 teaspoons chili sauce
1 tablespoon soy or groundnut oil	1 tablespoon soy or peanut oil

1

Thoroughly mash the beans with their salted sauce.

2

Mix in the tamari or shoyu sauce, chilli sauce and oil.

Note: Not suitable for freezing.

SWEET AND SOUR SAUCE

China

Serve this with stir-fried and stir-braised vegetables and with rice dishes. It can also be poured over plain fried bean curd.

Imperial (Metric)	American
1 medium carrot	1 medium carrot
1 tablespoon Chinese pickled vegetables	1 tablespoon Chinese pickled vegetables
3 tablespoons tomato paste	3 tablespoons tomato paste
2 tablespoons tamari or shoyu sauce	2 tablespoons tamari or shoyu sauce
¼ pint (150ml) pineapple juice	⅔ cup pineapple juice
2 tablespoons white wine vinegar	2 tablespoons white wine vinegar
2 tablespoons Chinese rice wine or dry sherry	2 tablespoons Chinese rice wine or dry sherry
1 tablespoon arrowroot	1 tablespoon arrowroot
4 tablespoons water	4 tablespoons water
1 tablespoon groundnut oil	1 tablespoon peanut oil

1

Cut the carrot into very thin matchstick pieces. Finely chop the pickles.

2

Mix together the tomato paste, tamari or shoyu sauce, pineapple juice, vinegar and wine or sherry.

3

Put the arrowroot in a bowl and mix in the water.

4

Heat the oil in a wok or large frying pan over high heat. Put in the carrot, and stir-fry 1 minute. Add the pickles and stir-fry a further minute.

5

Pour in the mixture of liquid ingredients, and bring to a boil.

6

Add the arrowroot mixture, and stir until the sauce thickens.

Note: Not suitable for freezing.

HOT MARINATING SAUCE

China

This sauce is used to flavour vegetables which are to be either stir-fried or deep-fried in a final cooking process. The amounts below make about 1½ pints (850ml or 3¾ cups).

The finished sauce, once cooled, can be stored in a covered container in the refrigerator. If it is used twice a week, it can be kept useable for up to two months. After you have used it, cool it. Line a sieve with muslin or with an old, washed-out, thin tea towel. Pour boiling water through it to scald it. Pour the sauce through the lined sieve into a bowl. Cool the sauce before putting it back into the refrigerator.

Imperial (Metric)	*American*
¾ pint (425ml) vegetable stock	2 cups vegetable stock
¼ pint (140ml) tamari or shoyu sauce	⅔ cup tamari or shoyu sauce
4 tablespoons Chinese rice wine or dry sherry	4 tablespoons Chinese rice wine or dry sherry
1 tablespoon black bean paste	1 tablespoon black bean paste
1 tablespoon hoisin sauce	1 tablespoon hoisin sauce
½ ounce (15g) fresh ginger root, peeled and finely chopped	½ ounce fresh ginger, peeled and finely chopped
4 medium onions, thinly sliced	4 medium onions, thinly sliced
2 garlic cloves, crushed	2 garlic cloves, crushed
¼ teaspoon five-spice powder	¼ teaspoon five-spice powder
¼ teaspoon ground black pepper	¼ teaspoon ground black pepper
2 ounces (55g) haricot beans, soaked overnight and drained	⅓ cup haricot beans, soaked overnight and drained
2 ounces (55g) peanuts	⅓ cup peanuts
4 dried Chinese mushrooms	⅓ cup Chinese mushrooms
4 ounces (115g) carrots, roughly chopped	1 medium carrot, roughly chopped
1 small white turnip, roughly chopped	1 small white turnip, roughly chopped
½ pint (285ml) water	1⅓ cups water

1

Put the stock, tamari or shoyu sauce, wine or sherry, soya paste, hoisin sauce, ginger root, onions, garlic, five-spice powder and pepper in a saucepan. Bring to a boil.

2

Add the remaining ingredients, and bring to a boil again.

3

Cover and simmer very gently for 1 hour, 30 minutes.

4

Strain the sauce as above. Cool, and put it in a covered container. Store it in the refrigerator.

SZECHUAN PEPPER AND SALT MIXTURE

China

This can be used as a seasoning for stir-fried or stir-braised vegetable dishes and for other sauces. It can also be used as a dip for deep-fried foods.

Imperial (Metric)	American
2 tablespoons Szechuan peppercorns	2 tablespoons Szechuan peppercorns
1 tablespoon fine sea salt	1 tablespoon fine sea salt

1

Heat a heavy frying pan over medium heat, without fat or water. Put in the peppercorns and stir for 2 minutes.

2

Put in the salt and continue stirring for 1 minute.

3

Using a large pestle and mortar, crush the pepper and salt together.

SWEET-SOUR
VEGETABLE SAUCE

China

Serve this with bean curd or egg dishes or with stir-fried or stir-braised single vegetables.

Imperial (Metric)	American
1 green pepper	1 sweet green pepper
3 ounces (85g) drained, tinned bamboo shoots	½ cup drained, canned bamboo shoots
3 ounces (85g) carrots	1 small carrot
2 fresh green or red chillies	2 fresh green or red chilis
2 tomatoes	2 tomatoes
1 tablespoon arrowroot	1 tablespoon arrowroot
6 fl ounces (175ml) water	¾ cup water
2 tablespoons Chinese rice wine or dry sherry	2 tablespoons Chinese rice wine or dry sherry
2 tablespoons white wine vinegar	2 tablespoons white wine vinegar
1 tablespoon honey	1 tablespoon honey
2 tablespoons tamari or shoyu sauce	2 tablespoons tamari or shoyu sauce
4 tablespoons Chinese pickled vegetables	4 tablespoons Chinese pickled vegetables

1

Core and seed the pepper, and cut it into matchstick pieces. Cut the bamboo shoots and carrots into matchstick pieces. Core, seed and finely chop the chillies. Scald, skin and chop the tomatoes. Put the arrowroot in a bowl, and mix in 4 tablespoons water, the wine or sherry and the vinegar.

2

Put the remaining water in a saucepan, and bring it to a boil. Add the honey and tamari or shoyu sauce. When the honey has dissolved, stir in the arrowroot mixture. Stir until the mixture thickens.

3

Put in the pepper, bamboo shoots, carrots, chillies, tomatoes and pickles. Simmer, uncovered, for 5 minutes.

Note: Not suitable for freezing.

AUBERGINE (EGGPLANT) SAMBAL

Indonesia

Imperial (Metric)	American
8 ounces (225g) aubergines	1¼ cups eggplant, diced
1 tablespoon sea salt	1 tablespoon sea salt
6 ounces (170g) tomatoes	1 medium tomato
4 garlic cloves	4 garlic cloves
1 tablespoon tomato ketchup	1 tablespoon ketchup
1 large onion	1 large onion
1 tablespoon groundnut oil	1 tablespoon peanut oil
2 teaspoons chilli powder	2 teaspoons chili powder
1 teaspoon Barbados sugar	1 teaspoon brown sugar

1

Cut the aubergine (eggplant) into ½-inch (1.5 cm) dice. Put into a colander, and sprinkle with the salt. Let drain for 20 minutes. Wash by running cold water through them. Dry with paper towels.

2

Scald, skin, seed and chop the tomatoes. Crush the garlic. Mix it with the tomato ketchup. Finely chop the onion.

3

Heat the oil in a wok or large frying pan over low heat. Put in the onion, and cook it until it begins to brown. Add the garlic mixture, chilli powder and sugar. Stir for 30 seconds.

4

Mix in the aubergine (eggplant) and tomatoes. Cover and simmer for 5 minutes. Transfer the contents of the pan to a pudding basin. Cover with foil.

5

Bring a pan of water to a boil. Lower in the basin. Cover and steam the mixture 20 minutes.

6

Serve hot or cold.

Note: Not suitable for freezing.

HOT BLACK BEAN AND TOMATO SAUCE

China

Serve this with Chinese egg dishes, with rice and with plain stir-fried or stir-braised vegetables.

Imperial (Metric)	American
8 ounces (225g) aubergines	1¼ cups eggplant, diced
1 tablespoon sea salt	1 tablespoon sea salt
8 ounces (225g) courgettes	1 cup zucchini, diced
4 tomatoes	4 tomatoes
1 red chilli	1 red chilli
1 medium onion	1 medium onion
4 tablespoons groundnut oil	4 tablespoons peanut oil
½ tablespoon salted black beans	½ tablespoon salted black beans
2 garlic cloves, crushed	2 garlic cloves, crushed
½ ounce (15g) fresh root ginger, peeled and grated	½ ounce fresh ginger, peeled and grated
6 fl ounces (175ml) vegetable stock	¾ cup vegetable stock
4 tablespoons Chinese rice wine or dry sherry	4 tablespoons Chinese rice wine or dry sherry
1 tablespoon hoisin sauce	1 tablespoon hoisin sauce
1 tablespoon sesame oil	1 tablespoon sesame oil

1

Cut the aubergines (eggplants) into ½-inch (1.5 cm) dice. Put them into a colander and sprinkle with the sea salt. Let drain for 20 minutes. Run cold water through them, and dry them with paper towels.

2

Cut the courgettes (zucchini) into ½-inch (2.5 cm) dice. Scald, skin and chop the tomatoes. Core, seed and finely chop the chilli. Finely chop the onion.

3

Heat the oil in a wok or large frying pan over medium heat. Put in the black beans, onion, garlic and ginger. Stir-fry for 2 minutes.

Note: Not suitable for freezing.

4

Add the aubergines (eggplant), courgettes (zucchini) and tomatoes, and stir-fry for 5 minutes over low heat.

5

Add the vegetable stock, wine or sherry and hoisin sauce. Cover and simmer very gently for 30 minutes.

6

Stir in the sesame oil.

SOYA SAMBAL

Indonesia

This is often served with rice dishes.

Imperial (Metric)	American
4 tablespoons tamari or shoyu sauce	4 tablespoons tamari or shoyu sauce
Juice of 2 limes (or 1 large lemon)	Juice of 2 limes (or 1 large lemon)
½ teaspoon chilli powder	½ teaspoon chili powder
4 shallots or very small onions, thinly sliced	4 shallots or very small onions, thinly sliced
1 garlic clove, crushed	1 garlic clove, crushed
2 tablespoons boiling water	2 tablespoons boiling water

1

Mix all the ingredients together well. Cool to room temperature if the water is still warm.

Note: Not suitable for freezing.

HOT YELLOW BEAN SAMBAL

Indonesia

Imperial (Metric)	American
One 6-ounce (170g) tin salted yellow beans	One 6-ounce can salted yellow beans
4 garlic cloves, crushed	4 garlic cloves, crushed
3 green chillies or	3 green chilis or
1 teaspoon chilli powder	1 teaspoon chili powder
1 medium onion	1 medium onion
½ ounce (15g) fresh ginger root	½ ounce fresh ginger
½ ounce (15g) tamarind	½ ounce tamarind
8 fl ounces (225ml) boiling water	1 cup boiling water
2 tablespoons groundnut oil	2 tablespoons peanut oil
1 teaspoon Barbados sugar	1 teaspoon brown sugar

1

Put the beans in a blender or food processor with the garlic. Work to a rough paste.

2

Core, seed and chop the chillies.

3

Finely chop the onion.

4

Peel and grate the ginger root.

5

Put the tamarind in a bowl. Pour the boiling water into it and leave it for 10 minutes. Rub it through a sieve.

6

Heat the oil in a wok or large frying pan over low heat. Put in the onion, and cook for 1 minute.

7

Put in the chillies and ginger, and stir 1 minute.

8

Add the bean and garlic paste, tamarind water and sugar. Stir and simmer, uncovered, for 10 minutes, stirring once after about 8 minutes.

Note: The sambal can be served hot or cold. If put into an airtight container it will keep in the refrigerator for up to one month.

 PEANUT SAMBAL

Indonesia

Imperial (Metric)	American
½ ounce (15g) peanuts	2 tablespoons peanuts
1 garlic clove	1 garlic clove
¼ teaspoon chilli powder	¼ teaspoon chili powder
3 tablespoons white wine vinegar	3 tablespoons white wine vinegar
¼ teaspoon Barbados sugar	¼ teaspoon brown sugar
1 tablespoon boiling water	1 tablespoon boiling water

1

Put the peanuts in a heavy saucepan. Set over medium heat, and stir until they begin to brown and smell very nutty, about 2 minutes. Remove from the heat, and tip them on to a plate to cool.

2

Crush the garlic with the chilli powder.

3

Put the nuts in a blender and grind finely.

4

Add the garlic and chilli mixture, vinegar, sugar and water. Grind together.

Note: Not suitable for freezing.

COCONUT SAMBAL

Indonesia

Imperial (Metric)	American
½ fresh coconut	½ fresh coconut
1 fresh red chilli	1 fresh red chili
1 tablespoon tamari or shoyu sauce	1 tablespoon tamari or shoyu sauce
1 garlic clove, crushed with pinch sea salt	1 garlic clove, crushed with pinch sea salt
½ small onion, finely chopped	½ small onion, finely chopped
Juice of 1 lime	Juice of 1 lime

1

Grate the coconut. Core, seed and finely chop the chilli.

2

Mix all the ingredients together.

3

Leave the sambal to stand for 30 minutes before serving.

Note: Not suitable for freezing.

SATAY SAUCE

Indonesia

Serve this with plainly cooked vegetables, with rice and with eggs.

Imperial (Metric)	American
1 medium onion, finely chopped	1 medium onion, finely chopped
5 macadamia nuts or ground almonds	5 macadamia nuts or ground almonds
4 ounces (115g) crunchy peanut butter	1 cup crunchy peanut butter
½ teaspoon chilli powder	½ teaspoon chili powder
1 tablespoon groundnut oil	1 tablespoon peanut oil
6 fl ounces (175ml) thin coconut milk	¾ cup thin coconut milk
2 tablespoons tamari or shoyu sauce	2 tablespoons tamari or shoyu sauce
Juice of ½ lime or 2 tablespoons lemon juice	Juice ½ lime or 2 tablespoons lemon juice

1

Put the onion, macadamia nuts or almonds, peanut butter, chilli powder and oil in a blender or food processor. Work to a thick paste.

2

Heat a wok over medium heat. Put in the paste, and stir for 2 minutes.

3

Pour in the coconut milk and simmer, stirring frequently, until the sauce thickens slightly.

4

Stir in the tamari or shoyu sauce and lime juice and reheat if necessary.

5

Serve hot.

Note: Not suitable for freezing.

PICKLED PINEAPPLE

Malaysia

This can be served with a spiced or curried main dish. It will keep in the refrigerator in a covered container for up to 3 days.

Imperial (Metric)	American
1 medium pineapple	1 medium pineapple
4 green chillies or	4 green chilis or
2 teaspoons chilli powder	2 teaspoons chili powder
¼ ounce (15g) mustard seeds	2 tablespoons mustard seeds
½ ounce (15g) fresh ginger root	½ ounce fresh ginger
8 fl ounces (225ml) white wine vinegar	1 cup white wine vinegar
¼ teaspoon sea salt (optional)	¼ teaspoon sea salt (optional)

1

Cut the husk from the pineapple. Dice the flesh, removing the core.

2

Core, seed and finely chop the chillies.

3

Coarsely crush the mustard seeds with a pestle and mortar. If you are using chilli powder, crush it with the mustard seeds.

4

Peel and grate the ginger root.

5

Put the mustard (and chilli powder if using) into a bowl. Gradually mix in the vinegar.

6

Stir in the pineapple, green chillies and ginger. Add salt if needed, and mix well.

7

Serve the pickle right away if wished or store it (see above).

Chapter 10
Desserts and Sweetmeats

Although the eastern world has a wide and varied range of savoury dishes, there are really only a few desserts.

The Japanese prefer to end the meal with a savoury and the Southeast Asians with fresh fruit. The Chinese have slightly more sweet recipes, but some of these such as the Sweet Green Pea Cubes, Sesame Seed Twists, Almond Biscuits and Thousand Layer Cake are finger foods rather than desserts to be eaten with a spoon.

The following recipes are those most suited to western kitchens and western habits and should be a fitting end to your meal.

ALMOND BISCUITS

China

Imperial (Metric)	American
6 ounces (170g) wholewheat flour	1½ cups whole wheat flour
Pinch of fine sea salt	Pinch of fine sea salt
½ teaspoon bicarbonate of soda	¼ teaspoon baking soda
3 ounces (85g) vegetable margarine	¾ cup vegetable margarine
1 ounce (30g) ground almonds	1½ tablespoons ground almonds
3 ounces (85g) honey	¼ cup honey
1 egg	1 egg
½ teaspoon almond essence	½ teaspoon almond essence
15 blanched almonds	15 blanched almonds
1 egg yolk beaten with 1 tablespoon water	1 egg yolk beaten with 1 tablespoon water

1

Heat the oven to 350F/180C/gas 4.

2

Put the flour in a mixing bowl, and toss in the salt and bicarbonate of soda (baking soda). Rub in the margarine. Mix in the ground almonds. Rub in the honey. Make a well in the centre. Add the egg and almond essence. Mix well. Knead in the bowl to make a pliable dough.

3

Make the dough into fifteen small balls. Lay them on a floured baking sheet and flatten to a thickness of ¼ inch (6 mm).

4

Press a blanched almond into the centre of each biscuit. Brush the biscuits with the egg yolk and water mixture.

5

Bake for 15 minutes.

Note: Not suitable for freezing.

SESAME TWISTS

China

Imperial (Metric)	American
2 tablespoons sesame seeds	2 tablespoons sesame seeds
8 ounces (225g) wholewheat flour	2 cups whole wheat flour
1 teaspoon bicarbonate of soda	1 teaspoon baking soda
½ ounce (15g) vegetable margarine	1 tablespoon vegetable margarine
2 ounces (55g) honey	1½ tablespoon honey
4 tablespoons water	4 tablespoons water
Oil for deep-frying	Oil for deep-frying

1

Put the sesame seeds in a heavy frying pan. Set over moderate heat, and stir until they brown and begin to jump. Tip out on to a plate to cool.

2

Put the flour and bicarbonate of soda (baking soda) in a mixing bowl. Rub in the margarine, and mix in the honey and sesame seeds. Add the water, and mix to make a soft dough.

3

Turn the dough on to a floured worktop and knead lightly. Roll to a thickness of ⅛ inch (3 mm). Cut into 1-by 2-inch (2.5-by-5cm) rectangles. Make a lengthways slit in the centre of each strip. Bring one end of the strip through to form a twist.

4

Heat a pan of deep oil to 325F/160C. Deep-fry the twists, four at a time, until golden brown, about 2 minutes. Drain on paper towels.

5

Serve hot or cold.

Note: Freeze separately on trays. Store in the freezer in a polythene (plastic) bag for up to 2 months. Thaw at room temperature.

HONEYED PASTRIES

China

Imperial (Metric)	American
12 ounces (340g) wholewheat flour	3 cups whole wheat flour
2 teaspoons bicarbonate of soda	2 teaspoons baking soda
3 eggs, beaten	3 eggs, beaten
4 tablespoons water	4 tablespoons water
Oil for deep-frying	Oil for deep-frying
Syrup:	Syrup:
8 fl ounces (225ml) water	1 cup water
6 ounces (170ml) honey	$\frac{1}{3}$ cup honey

1

Put the flour on to a work surface, and scatter the bicarbonate of soda (baking soda) over the top. Make a well in the centre. Pour in the eggs and water. Using your hands, gradually mix the eggs into the flour and then knead until you have a smooth dough.

2

Roll the dough to a thickness of $\frac{1}{8}$ inch (3 mm). cut it into strips about $\frac{3}{4}$ by 2 inches (2 by 5 cm).

3

Heat a pan of deep oil to 375F/190C. Drop the pieces of dough into the oil about ten at a time. Deep-fry for 45 seconds or until golden. Remove, and drain on paper towels.

4

Put the water and honey in a saucepan and stir over low heat until the honey dissolves. Boil for 2 minutes. Mix in all the deep-fried dough strips, and stir until each one is evenly coated with syrup.

5

Turn the strips and syrup into a flat dish. Leave until completely cold.

6

Serve as sweetmeats after a meal.

Note: Best eaten on day of cooking. Two to four tablespoons of sesame seeds can be added to the syrup.

SWEET GREEN PEA CUBES

China

Imperial (Metric)	American
8 ounces (225g) split green peas	1 cup split green peas
1 pint (570ml) water	2½ cups water
3 ounces (85g) honey	¼ cup honey
3 tablespoons arrowroot mixed	3 tablespoons arrowroot mixed
with 3 fl ounces (90ml) water	with ⅓ cup water

1

Soak the peas in the water for 4 hours.

2

Put the peas and the water in a saucepan. Bring to a boil, cover, and simmer for 45 minutes or until they are soft.

3

Rub the peas and any remaining liquid through a fine sieve. Return the mixture to the cleaned pan.

4

Stir in the honey and the arrowroot mixture.

5

Bring the mixture to a boil, stirring. Turn the heat to the lowest setting and cook, stirring, for 10 minutes.

6

Pour the mixture into a lightly oiled shallow dish so that it is about 1 inch (2.5 cm) deep. Chill for 1 hour or until it becomes very firm.

7

Cut the pea cake into cubes. Pile the cubes in a pyramid on a plate.

Note: These cubes are served as sweetmeats after a meal. Each person spears his or her own from the plate using a cocktail stick (toothpick). Not suitable for freezing.

WATERMELON BASKET

China

Imperial (Metric)	American
1 medium-sized watermelon	1 medium-sized watermelon
1 small cantaloupe melon	1 small cantaloupe
2 oranges	2 oranges
3 peaches	3 peaches
6 ounces (170g) red cherries	1 cup red cherries
One 8-ounce (225g) tin lychees, drained	One 8-ounce can lychees, drained
¼ pint (140ml) sweet sherry	⅔ cup sweet sherry
2 tablespoons clear honey	2 tablespoons clear honey
5 ounces (140g) black grapes in one bunch	¼ pound black grapes in one bunch

1

Make a cut in the watermelon from the top end, down the centre to ½ inch (1.5 cm) away from the centre. Make a similar cut from the base. Then cut round half the circumference of the melon from either end of the first cut. Remove the wedge of melon that is now cut away. Repeat on the other side so that you are left with a basket shape with a 1-inch (2.5 cm) wide handle.

2

Using a Parisienne scoop (melon baller), scoop out all the pink flesh of the watermelon, discarding the seeds as you do so.

3

Cut the cantaloupe melon in half. Remove the seeds and scoop the flesh into balls.

4

Cut the rind and pith from the oranges. Cut the segments away from the skin. Stone (pit) the peaches and cut them into thin, lengthways slices. Stone (pit) the cherries.

5

Put the prepared fresh fruit plus the drained lychees into a bowl. Pour in the sherry and spoon in the honey. Gently turn the fruits. Leave them for 30 minutes in the refrigerator.

6

Put the melon basket on to a serving plate. Fill it with the fruits. Hang the bunch of grapes from the handle.

Note: Not suitable for freezing.

PEKING DUST

China

Imperial (Metric)	American
12 ounces (340g) unsweetened chestnut puree	2¼ cups unsweetened chestnut puree
¼ teaspoon fine sea salt	¼ teaspoon fine sea salt
3 ounces (85g) honey	¼ cup honey
½ pint (285ml) double cream	1¼ cups heavy cream
¼ teaspoon vanilla essence	¼ teaspoon vanilla essence
4 glacé cherries	4 glacé cherries
8 small pieces candied angelica	8 small pieces candied angelica

1

Put the chestnut puree in a bowl. Add the salt and honey, and beat to make a smooth paste. Divide the chestnut paste between four small bowls.

2

Stiffly whip the cream. Add the vanilla essence, and whip lightly again.

3

Pile or pipe the cream on top of the chestnut paste. Top it with a glacé cherry and two pieces of angelica.

Note: For convenience, use tinned (canned) chestnut puree. If you wish to use fresh chestnuts, you will need 1 pound (455g). Slit the tops. Boil for 30 minutes. Drain, skin and mash them. Not suitable for freezing.

THOUSAND LAYER CAKE

China

Imperial (Metric)	American
1½ pounds (680g) wholewheat flour	6 cups whole wheat flour
6 ounces (170g) Barbados sugar	¾ cup brown sugar
1½ ounces (40g) fresh yeast or 1 tablespoon dried	2 tablespoons fresh yeast or 1 tablespoon dried
¾ pint (425ml) warm water	2 cups warm water
4 ounces (115g) vegetable margarine	1 cup vegetable margarine
2 ounces (55g) shelled walnuts, crushed or ground	½ cup shelled walnuts, crushed or ground

1

Put the flour in a mixing bowl, and mix in the sugar. Make a well in the centre.

2

Sprinkle the yeast in the warm water. Pour it in the flour. Mix everything to a dough. Turn it on to a floured work surface, and knead well for about 5 minutes or until smooth. Return to the bowl. Cover the bowl with a clean tea towel, and leave in a warm place for 3 hours or until the dough has doubled in size.

4

Divide the dough into three. Roll each piece into a rectangle 8 by 12 inches (20 by 30 cm).

5

Spread on one sixth of the vegetable margarine, and sprinkle on one sixth of the walnuts over one portion of the dough. Put another portion on top. Spread a further sixth of the margarine, and sprinkle over a further one sixth of the walnuts and top with the third portion.

6

Roll out the dough layers to a large rectangle 12 by 30 inches, (30 by 75 cm). Spread one sixth of the remaining margarine and walnuts over two thirds of the surface. Fold over the other third. Spread a further sixth over that. Turn the dough so that the folded edge is toward you. Repeat the rolling and spreading twice more, without rolling for the final time. You should finish with folded layers of pastry about 8 by 12 inches (20 by 30 cm).

7

Wrap the finished cake in a clean tea towel. Put it in a steamer. Lower the steamer over boiling water, and steam the cake 1 hour.

8

Cool the cake completely. Serve it cut into slices.

Note: Not suitable for freezing.

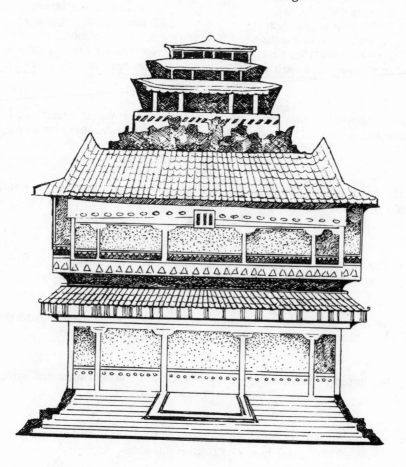

ALMOND JELLY WITH MANDARINS

China

Imperial (Metric)	American
4 ounces (115g) almonds	1 cup almonds
¾ pint (425ml) water	2 cups water
¼ pint (140ml) evaporated milk	⅔ cup evaporated milk
1 ounce (30g) honey	1 tablespoon honey
3 tablespoons agar-agar	3 tablespoons agar-agar
¼ teaspoon almond essence	¼ teaspoon almond essence
Two 8-ounce (225g) tins mandarin oranges in fruit juice	Two 8-ounce cans mandarin oranges in fruit juice

1

Put the almonds in a saucepan, and cover them with water. Bring to a boil. Drain, and squeeze them from their skins. Finely grind them by using a blender, food processor or coffee grinder.

2

Put the ground almonds in a saucepan with the water. Bring them gently to a boil, and take the pan from the heat. Leave the almonds for 30 minutes.

3

Strain the almonds through fine muslin or a clean tea towel, squeezing to extract as much liquid as possible. Discard the almonds.

4

Put the almond liquid in a saucepan with the evaporated milk. Add the honey, and stir over low heat until it has dissolved.

5

Bring the liquid to just below boiling point. Add the agar-agar and stir for 2 minutes to dissolve it.

6

Pour the mixture into an oiled, shallow dish. Leave it in the refrigerator for 2 hours or until it has set.

7

Quickly dip the base of the mould into hot water. Turn out the jelly and cut it into diamond shapes.

8

Put the mandarins and their juice into a large serving bowl. Mix in the cubes of jelly.

Note: If wished, the jelly can be made with ready-ground almonds. Not suitable for freezing.

PLUM BLOSSOM AND SNOW

China

Imperial (Metric)	American
2 dessert apples	2 dessert apples
2 bananas	2 bananas
2 eggs, separated	2 eggs, separated
2 ounces (55g) Barbados sugar	¼ cup brown sugar
2 tablespoons arrowroot	2 tablespoons arrowroot
3 tablespoons milk	3 tablespoons milk
2 tablespoons water	2 tablespoons water

1

Heat the oven to 425F/220C/Gas mark 7.

2

Peel and core the apples, and cut them into thin lengthways slices. Peel and thinly slice the bananas. Mix the apples and bananas in a heatproof dish.

3

Beat the egg yolks lightly. Mix in the sugar, arrowroot, milk and water. Put the mixture in a saucepan, and stir it over a low heat, without boiling, until it is smooth and thick. Pour it over the apples and bananas.

4

Stiffly whip the egg whites and spoon them over the top.

5

Bake for about 5 minutes or until the egg whites are beginning to brown. Serve hot.

Note: The apples and bananas will be just heated through and not softened, giving the fresh flavours of raw fruits combined in a rich liquid and with a light and fluffy top. Not suitable for freezing.

SWIMMING MELON

Laos

Imperial (Metric)	American
1 honeydew melon	1 honeydew melon
4 fl ounces (125ml) thin coconut milk, cold but not set	½ cup thin coconut milk, cold but not set
4 fl ounces (125ml) thick coconut milk, cold but not set	½ cup thick coconut milk, cold but not set
2 ounces (55g) Barbados sugar	¼ cup brown sugar

1

Cut the melon in half, and scoop away the seeds. Slice the melon and cut away the rind. Cut the flesh into small, thin strips.

2

Mix the thin coconut milk with the sugar, stirring until the sugar has almost dissolved.

3

Mix the melon into the sugar mixture.

4

Divide the melon among four small bowls or glasses. Top with the remaining coconut milk.

Note: Not suitable for freezing.

SOUP-POT COCONUT DESSERT CAKE

Laos

The name of this recipe comes from the fact that it is often cooked in a dry, covered pot in an improvised oven. Hot charcoal is lit in a brazier and is then removed. The covered pot is put inside the brazier and the charcoal heaped on top. It works perfectly well in a conventional oven.

Imperial (Metric)	American
2 ounces (55g) wholewheat flour	½ cup whole wheat flour
¼ teaspoon fine sea salt	¼ teaspoon fine sea salt
½ teaspoon bicarbonate of soda	½ teaspoon baking soda
6 ounces (170g) Barbados sugar	¾ cup brown sugar
12 fl ounces (340ml) thick coconut milk	1½ cups thick coconut milk
5 eggs, beaten	5 eggs, beaten

1

Heat the oven to 350F/180C/gas 4.

2

Put the flour in a bowl with the salt and bicarbonate of soda (baking soda) and sugar.

3

Gradually beat in the coconut milk and eggs.

4

Pour the mixture into a shallow, ovenproof dish. Bake for 40 minutes or until it has risen and browned.

Note: This is not really like a cake but more like a sweet custard, and should be served straight from the dish. It rises considerably during baking but falls equally quickly as it cools. If you are going to eat it hot therefore, serve it as soon as it comes out of the oven. However, it tastes equally good cold. Not suitable for freezing.

PUMPKIN IN COCONUT MILK

Indonesia

Imperial (Metric)	American
1 pound (455g) pumpkin (weighed after seeds and rind removed)	1 pound pumpkin (weighed after seeds and rind are removed)
¾ pint (425ml) thick coconut milk	2 cups thick coconut milk
3 ounces (85g) honey	¼ cup honey
Pinch of salt	Pinch of salt

1

Cut the pumpkin into ¾-inch (2 cm) dice. Bring a pan of water to a boil. Put in the pumpkin, and cook for 10 minutes. Drain.

2

Put the coconut milk in a saucepan, and stir in the honey. Stir over low heat, without boiling, until the honey has dissolved.

3

Put in the pumpkin, and simmer gently for 20 minutes or until soft.

4

Serve warm.

Note: Not suitable for freezing.

SWEET POTATOES IN COCONUT MILK

Indonesia

Make the same as for Pumpkin in Coconut Milk (above) using 1 pound (455g) peeled, sweet potatoes. Barbados (brown) sugar may be used instead of honey.

COCONUT-FILLED PANCAKES

Indonesia

Imperial (Metric)	American
Pancake Batter:	Pancake Batter:
4 ounces (115g) wholewheat flour	1 cup whole wheat flour
Pinch of sea salt	Pinch of sea salt
1 egg	1 egg
1 egg yolk	1 egg yolk
¼ pint (140ml) milk	⅓ cup milk
¼ pint (140ml) water	⅓ cup water
1 tablespoon groundnut oil	1 tablespoon peanut oil
Oil for frying	Oil for frying
Filling:	Filling:
½ fresh coconut	½ fresh coconut
8 fl ounces (225ml) water	1 cup water
2 ounces (55g) Barbados sugar	¼ cup brown sugar
4-inch (10 cm) cinnamon stick	4-inch cinnamon stick
Pinch of sea salt	Pinch of sea salt
Juice of ½ lime or 2 tablespoons lemon juice	Juice of ½ lime or 2 tablespoons lemon juice

1

Make the batter. Put the flour and salt into a bowl, and make a well in the centre. Put in the egg and egg yolk. Beat them with a little flour from the sides of the well. Mix together the milk and water. Beat half the mixture into the flour. Beat in the oil and finally the remaining milk and water mixture. Let the batter stand in a cool place for 30 minutes.

2

Finely grate the coconut.

3

Put the water and sugar in a saucepan, and stir over a low heat until the sugar is dissolved. Stir in the coconut, and add the cinnamon stick and salt. Bring to a boil, and then simmer for 15 minutes or until the coconut has soaked up all the water. Add the lime or lemon juice. Stir for 1 minute on the heat. Remove the cinnamon stick, and keep the filling warm.

4

To make the pancakes, heat 1 tablespoon oil in a frying pan over high heat. Put in 3 tablespoons of the pancake batter, and tip the pan to spread it out into a pancake. Cook until the underside is speckled brown. Turn the pancake over and cook the other side. Slip the pancake on to a plate and keep it warm. Cook the others in the same way. This should make 8 pancakes.

5

Roll up a portion of the filling in each pancake before serving.

Note: The filling is not suitable for freezing. The pancakes can be frozen with layers of greaseproof paper in between them and can be stored for up to two months. Thaw them at room temperature, and reheat them in a low oven.

EIGHT-TREASURE RICE PUDDING

China

This is the most celebrated of all Chinese sweet dishes and is served at the Chinese New Year celebrations. It is named after the eight treasures that in Chinese legend were supposed to have mystical powers. These are the dragon pearl, the golden coin, the lozenge, the mirror, the stone chime, books, rhinocerous horns and artemesia leaf. The pudding must contain at least eight ingredients. In China it is made with a sticky polished rice called glutinous rice, but brown rice works very well.

Imperial (Metric)	American
8 ounces (225g) short-grain brown rice	1 cup short-grain brown rice
1½ ounce (40g) vegetable margarine	2 tablespoons vegetable margarine
1 ounce (30g) Barbados sugar	1 tablespoon brown sugar
10 Chinese red dates, halved and stoned	10 Chinese red dates, halved and stoned
30 large raisins	30 large raisins
2 ounces (55g) candied orange peel, cut into strips	2 ounces candied orange peel, cut into strips
2 ounces (55g) almonds, blanched	½ cup almonds, blanched
10 maraschino cherries	10 maraschino cherries
4 Chinese figs, halved	4 Chinese figs, halved
8 ounces (225g) Red Bean Paste (page 172)	1 cup Red Bean Paste (page 172)

1

Put the rice in a saucepan. Pour on 1 pint (570ml or 2½ cups) boiling water. Cover and simmer for 45 minutes or until the rice is soft and all the water has been absorbed. Mix in 1 ounce (30g or 2 tablespoons) margarine and the sugar.

2

Use the remaining margarine to thickly grease a 1½ pint (850ml or 3¾ cup) pudding basin.

3

Cover the base and sides of the greased basin with a thin layer of rice. Press fruits and nuts into the rice to make an attractive pattern that will show through when the rice is turned out.

4

Put in about one third of the remaining rice. If any fruit and nuts are left, arrange them on top of this. Put in all the red bean paste in a single, even layer. Cover it with the remaining rice.

5

Cover the pudding with greaseproof (waxed or parchment) paper and foil and tie this round with string. Bring a pan of water to a boil. Lower in the pudding, and steam it for 1 hour, never letting it come off the boil and adding more boiling water to the pan when necessary.

Note: Not suitable for freezing.

INDEX